SEMIOTEXT(E) FOREIGN AGENTS SERIES

The publication of this book was supported by the French Ministry of Foreign Affairs through the Cultural Services of the French Embassy, New York.

"Ouvrage publié avec le concours du Ministère français chargé de la Culture–Centre nationale du livre".

"What They Looked Like Photographed" published in "Sommes nous?" from the collective Tendance Floue, with the autorisation of Éditions Jean di Sciullo.

Published by Semiotext(e)
2007 Wilshire Blvd., Suite 427, Los Angeles, CA 90057
www.semiotexte.com

Special thanks to Robert Dewhurst.

Cover Photography by Jean Baudrillard
Backcover and inside photography by Jean Baudrillard
Design by Hedi El Kholti

ISBN-13: 978-1-58435-049-1
Distributed by The MIT Press, Cambridge, Mass. and London, England
Printed in the United States of America

# RADICAL
# ALTERITY

**Jean Baudrillard / Marc Guillaume**

Translated by Ames Hodges

**\<e\>**

# Contents

# Cool Thinking

"The only deep desire is the desire of the object. Not desire for something I am missing, or even for something (or someone) that misses me but for something that does not miss me at all, that is perfectly able to exist without me... The Other is the one who does not miss me, and that is radical alterity."[1] We could add: someone who not only does not miss me, but misses no one.

The object, in its silence and solitude without need or desire for others, brings a specific power of seduction into play. The object's genius lies there. It gives the object its secret—and objective—relationship with the photographic lens [*l'objectif*] and, by extension, with the subject that photographs it. That is why objects are the easiest things to photograph. "For objects, primitives and animals, alterity is certain; the most insignificant objects are 'other.' For subjects, it is much less certain." It then becomes necessary to make "beings more enigmatic for themselves, more foreign for each other. Thus the key to the photographic act is not to take them as objects but to make them become objects, to make them become others, to take them for what they are."

---

1. For Illusion and Reality are not Opposed...

The apparent absence of human subjects in the work of Jean Baudrillard is therefore, in fact, the reflection of a presence. Yet it is a presence without *aura*, the presence of a being preserved in both his or her banality and alterity, maintained in the enigma that gives them their power of seduction.

There is no condescension in dealing with the social in terms of masses: each person retains his or her freedom, enigma and solitude. The world according to Baudrillard is a world of objects and masses. Direct confrontation with human subjects is always eluded; they only appear shrouded in an objectal dignity that preserves their radical alterity. Objects and masses are the place where beings disappear but also where the Other appears. They are therefore the place where beings are faithful to themselves and where we can be faithful to them. In the refuge of the masses, as Jean Baudrillard represents it for us, every life is respectable, because every life is the center of the world.

"Only the inhuman is photogenic. Reciprocal stupefaction only works at this price, through our complicity with the world and the world's complicity with us."

These are fragments of Jean Baudrillard's text. Fragments selected at random, or almost. Fragments that we will not comment on, explain, contextualize or, worse, *systematize*. They are fragments we can take, deform and set in relation to other fragments. Or we can extenuate them, take them to their limit: doing this is not easy because Baudrillard's thought is never measured or nuanced—it is only ambivalent, which is very different. It is already pushed to the extreme.

If there is a correct way of using his texts, it is not to capture his thought but a *regime* of thought. A unique regime. Far from the genealogies and minute conceptual dissections of deconstruction, but not so far from the objectivizing practice of a certain type of photography. Something like *thought-feedback*, which is very different from image-feedback because this thought-feedback also involves turning and deviation. Reversed, *revealed* thought—present photographically in the passage from negative to positive—with an effervescence that finds its uniqueness in the process that created it.[2] *Cool thinking.*

"The world is beautiful like a cryptogram to decipher," wrote Mallarmé. Baudrillard's thought-feedback suggests that we make the world more beautiful by making it even more indecipherable. *Shadowing the world.* In praise of the shadow that doubles the world: "The world was given to us enigmatic and unintelligible, and the task of thought, if possible, is to make it even more enigmatic and even more unintelligible."[3] Jean Baudrillard could have put this statement of principle at the beginning of his book, but applying it to his own approach, he only unveils it at the end. We can imagine that many a naïve reader has entered the maze of one of his books—or all of his books—in an attempt to decipher the world, a world that seemed to belong to us in its very immediacy. Many readers get lost along the way; others misread him and only find apocalyptic or nihilist descriptions.

To avoid their mistakes, we must take his principle seriously. The world is given to us with no possible giving back and with no

---

2. Here is the art and pleasure of quotation like "decanting your thought through someone else, who returns it to you as if you had given it to him or her," *Cool Memories IV.*

3. *L'Échange impossible.*

responsibility of any kind, especially not the responsibility to explain it. Calculating and logical thought only serves to exploit the world while separating us from it. Sovereign thought, thought equal to the world, is comparable to the relationship poetry and music have with the world. "Without music, the world might have been a mistake" (Nietzsche). Baudrillard's works are composed like musical forms, with major themes, variations, refrains and silence.

## The Uncertainty Principle of Thought

Sovereign thought, which cannot be exchanged for anything, loses its grip and is destined for unyielding uncertainty. "The uncertainty of thought is that it cannot be exchanged for either truth or reality."[4] In this ellipsis, Baudrillard implicitly points to a unique position in philosophy.

Philosophy has always recognized that thought should not choose in itself the things about which we must think. The choice must be absolutely independent of thought and come from completely outside it. Philosophical tradition resolves this initial problem by first proposing a transcendent authority that it calls truth. But this truth, which is still unknown, receives a form from philosophers when they assume that thought is predestined for this form, able to recognize it and predisposed to loving it. Truth in this case is not completely foreign to thought and the circle that philosophical thought wanted to avoid closes again. A second approach states that men and women, to the extent that they claim to have a mind, think *naturally*: there is a necessity of the mind, like the

---

4. *Op. cit.*

bodily necessities of human beings and animals, that pushes them to seek the truth. Deleuze wrote in this regard that "philosophers readily assume that the mind as mind and thinkers as thinkers want the truth, love and desire the truth, seek the truth naturally. They grant themselves the goodwill of thought in advance." (*Proust and Signs*)

The preconceived "image" of thought permeates every philosophy up to Nietzsche, even though it is already partially contested in particular philosophies (like the cynics or Spinoza). This dominant form, which Deleuze calls dogmatic thought and Baudrillard calls critical thought, serves as a model for traditional philosophy that thinks that reality is rational and therefore "exchangeable" with thought. As Leon Chestov wrote: "'Reality is rational' is the essential axiom of any philosophy, at least of any philosophy that only seeks the possible."

It is likely that Chestov had a direct influence on Georges Bataille in his insistence on accentuating the limits of philosophy and the need for thinking beyond, or at least beyond dogmatic philosophy. Like Bataille, like Deleuze, like Derrida to some extent (for example when he defines deconstruction, in a lapidary statement, as "impossible"), Baudrillard joins a search for the impossible or for a philosophy of the event, of discontinuity *ex nihilo*: "Against the thinking of origins and endings, of evolution and continuity, a thinking of discontinuity." An event of the world, for which the Big Bang is the absolute model, but also event of life, of sexualized reproduction and death, of language "that long precedes us and turns around in us to think us"[5] (I would add to seduce us and invite us to play with it).

--------

5. *Op. cit.*

After Nietzsche, Bataille, Deleuze and a few others, Baudrillard invites us to shed critical thought, to forget "the ideas that change and multiply... (like) a history of ideas and their hypothetical finality." Forget Foucault, in an even more radical way than before.[6] Leave behind the authors who continue to produce more explanations and interpretations of the world and who must have read *The Gay Science* or *The Accursed Share* but continue to run around like chickens with their heads cut off.

## A Cartographer? No, a Writer

For this reason, we should avoid direct commentary of Jean Baudrillard's work or even using it as a pretext for a more personal analysis. And we should not separate his work into parts, by distinguishing for example a block of texts on objects and consumer society, another block on communication, another on seduction or the impossibility of exchange, etc.[7] There are, of course, different

---

6. Leaving the accumulation of knowledge to the historians, letting them autopsy the corpse of the past was Baudrillard's argument in this article that was thankfully developed into a short book called *Forget Foucault*.

7. It is possible, however, hypothetically speaking, to distinguish between a (chronological) first part of Baudrillard's work that runs up to *Symbolic Exchange and Death*, which is at least in part marked by the application of *critical* thought to different themes: consumer society, the media, a critique of Marx (*The Mirror of Production*). These remarkable essays marked their time, and while they were already permeated with the regime of thought that would follow, they remained connected to critical thought that gave their author the image of a sociologist. The same is not true of the texts that followed and reflected a radically different regime of thought.

themes but his writing always returns to the same questions. They are more than a main theme; the same position, the same operation and the same obsession haunt all of these themes.

The density of a work is one criterion among others but it is the most consistent trait that distinguishes the accumulation of knowledge in a university or disciplinary position from *writing* that takes its necessity from a position of gay science or disquiet. It would be particularly unwise to try to cloak this writing in a gloss, which is hard work in general and in Baudrillard's case completely inappropriate.

Jean Baudrillard is obviously not a sociologist in the University sense of the word. The little consideration shown for his work by academic authorities can only be seen as reasonable and mostly positive. We should not try to compensate for this fortunate oversight but be the *guardians of the freedom* that this work introduces into thought by saving it from restrictive reductions.

Should we go so far as to free the work from its author? "A book is finished when you can think that you have carried it as far as possible, with the knowledge of an impassable limit that only the book can cross or that some readers will take it to its end and even beyond its end."[8]

Why, how do we read Jean Baudrillard? What pleasure, what attraction, what impulse, what *laughter* do we find in his texts? (And sometimes, what profound shock: writing that does not disorient or contradict would not be a source of thought. There must be a flip side to jubilation, a flipside to laughter.) Why do we visit the mental world he creates out of the world we share? What joyous disquiet do we gain from these visits?

---

8. *Cool Memories IV.*

Or instead: Why are we seduced by this shadow given to the world?

It is not easy to speak of seduction with Jean Baudrillard… "Seduction is enigmatic… it cannot be spoken or revealed… it is unexplainable evidence." The quote is from a passage in *Fatal Strategies* where love and seduction are opposed. The passage is exceptionally instructive because the invention of the concept of seduction—and it is truly an invention—sheds light on our relationship with others. Radical alterity can only be respected in a relationship of seduction.

A re-enchantment of the world? I would not pick that word although it does sometimes apply. I would rather speak of freedom and lightness. Baudrillard frees us from the social world and the dogmatic representations with which it is often covered.[9] It releases the world and those who live in it from the duty of knowing more, always more and from the guilt of not knowing or understanding enough about it. So that the world can remain beautiful like a cryptogram hidden under the flows of information accumulated each day.[10] Deleuze wrote concerning Foulcault: "A writer? No, a cartographer." We could say the opposite of Jean Baudrillard: A cartographer? No, a writer. And every true writer has his or her own language and unique topology.

To bring the seductive power of the cryptogram into play, the point of view, the play of—harsh—light and preserved shadows. Then we can show the limits, the singular points, the hidden layers while protecting the enigma without which the world would lose

---

9. For example, in the early 1970s, he freed the social—and some of us by the same token—from the "mirror of production."

10. Why read or listen to the media, asked Fellini, "why absorb this daily poison?"

its beauty. The beauty of what *is*, without reason, in its absolute gratuitousness.

## Strange Attractors

Which leads us to the more general hypothesis that I made about the uniqueness of a regime of thought and the most important point: the mode of thinking is more important than the thought itself.

While this thinking is not up for interpretation, it nonetheless appears to be marked by the *figures* and oppositions of terms that give it a rigorous *form*. Figures of becoming, destiny, fatality (and metamorphosis) opposed to the figures of change and exchange, the fractal and the spectral (and metastasis.)

There are multiple operations at the origin of these figures, classic rhetorical operations no doubt, but also operations in the mathematical sense, basic geometrical transformations and tools of anamorphosis: reversion and ambivalence, exponentiation, exceedance, fractalization, doubling, ellipsis, *fading*, and disappearance.[11] In geometry, we once studied a strange operation, inversion,

---

11. Baudrillard's fascination with limit points, fault lines, singular objects or phenomena: the poles, the date line in the Pacific, black holes, the memory of water, phase changes, apoptosis as a juxtaposition of inverse processes. His way of applying the operations of the physical or biological world to the world of the masses is easy to explain but we must avoid oversimplification and preserve the seductive power of these metaphors. In the *Cool Memories* series, these operations (passing limits, reversion and self-reversion) produce amazing fragments most freely and directly.

that turned a circle into a straight line with infinite points. We must try to transfer that operation to the regime of thought: transforming the circles of stereotypes and critical thought into something totally different but with a rigorous and secret relationship to the original discourse.

We can advance in this line of thinking by making the hypothesis that Baudrillard's regime of thought is a search for *strange attractors*, the points of regions where the trajectories of complex, chaotic systems subject to variations in the initial conditions are forced to converge.[12] In the chaotic flux of virtual data, opinions and representations, Baudrillard finds *informational attractors* and then builds his own from them. In the flux and endless stock of preconceived ideas, false proof and one-track thinking, it is easy to pick out symptomatic accumulations and repetitions, especially symptoms of denial.[13] Starting with these points, you then take them to the extreme, inverse and multiply... counterfeiting Baudrillard's style brings you closer to it! Add all of the terms—the "passwords," the ones that led to a book of interviews[14]—that make up Baudrillard's conceptual topology (not cartography),

---

12. Like the image of a whirlpool in liquid drawn out through the hole in the bottom of a basin, or waters streaming down a valley into a single current. The first intuition of strange attractors can be found in Poincaré concerning the three body problem. The fractal nature and properties of strange attractors were discovered in 1971 by D. Ruelle and F. Takens.

13. As an example, the current repetition of the theme of sustainable development is the sign that it is not longer sustainable. And maybe the unmentionable wish to see the world destroyed with us or after us feeds our protests that we love our great-grandchildren.

14. *Passwords*.

that characterize his own attractors, his pass-concepts, and allow him to disorient the discourses we pronounce about the world.

These operations and attractors allow us to reorganize or disorganize everything related to identity, humanity, security, general good feelings and what Spinoza called the sad passions, but also the discourses on cloning, artificial intelligence, virtuality, networks, and globalization.

It is important for these operations to be reversible, self-reversible, and for the passwords to be organized in couples so that everything can be perceived and thought of reversibly. Or dually. Good and Evil. Saekina and Lilith (*The Intelligence of Evil or the Lucidity Pact*). Knowing how to inverse the positions allows for a subtle play with points of view that frees us from a representation of the world subject to causality and subjectivity. Thus objects see us, an old Lacanian and even Sartrean story; masses do not submit to power, but suffocate it ironically; adults become the potential victims of children; good health is threatened by the viruses that it creates... This reversibility or dual relationship is the condition for a distancing that sometimes allows secret hatred to appear, hatred that allows thought to discover what is in fact hidden under the thick layers of conventional thought and good intentions.[15]

These oppositions converge towards the central form of singularity (and also, again, the event) and therefore of impossible

---

15. An ability to grasp politics—for example what made Jean Baudrillard the inventor of the *Gauche divine* [Divine Left]—was made possible by this position of detestation.

exchange. Singularity comes from a double detachment: separating from the general is not enough—it is the trap of individualism and idiosyncrasy that are only singular relative to the masses like a grain of sand on a beach. It is a first, fractal level of singularity. Absolute singularity is a unique sign with no relation to the general and no possible exchange. Between the absolute singularities, there remains the possibility of a play of metamorphoses on the basis of the *inexistence* of their own being (think of Pessòa and his "wanting to be nothing" and his metamorphoses, of Sade declaring that "bodies can only be exchanged in the secret of signs.") Being in itself has a history woven from alienations and conquest; it has an illusory finality, the pretense to "become what it is." Only singularity has a becoming, the possibility of freely metamorphosing.

For "in another dimension, the dimension of destiny and becoming (where thought 'becomes'), there is only ever one idea: the sovereign hypothesis, equivalent to the sovereign passion of which Nietzsche spoke… [that] delivers us from all of the others, delivers us from plurality, from the frenzied exchange of modes of thought and modes of existence which is the caricature and simulacrum of becoming."[16]

This sovereign and unique idea, which haunts all of Baudrillard's writing after *Symbolic Exchange and Death*, is not to mention, or not entirely, no more than Nietzsche's sovereign idea, the Eternal Return. It remains partially secret, keeping an enigma to escape exchange and maintain a radical alterity of thought. Some madness as well: "Since the world is evolving towards a mad state of things, one must take a mad point of view towards it." Bataille adopted almost the same

---

16. Op. cit.

position at the end of *The Accursed Share*, while retaining the hypothesis of a reversal that would save the world.[17]

## Sovereign Thought

The essential remains to be said. For prudence's sake, I will try to be brief and allusive, following the suggestion and example of *Cool Memories*: "You will be judged on the brevity of your intuitions and your speech."

A body of work unflinchingly opposed to the processes of research and knowledge based on the illusory erasure of subjectivity

---

17. There is a heritage and a break between Bataille and Baudrillard. In *The Accursed Share*, Bataille wrote: "Human kind may have lost the world in leaving animality, but became the consciousness of having lost it that we are." Human beings are a separation that thinks and any attempt at objectification (rational thought), while giving us *utilitarian* mastery over the world, separates us even more from it by allotting us an *indignity* that Bataille reads into the representations of Lascaux where animals are magnified. Thought, because it is the product of an existence torn from the world, is negated in its objects and can only reach a radical, sovereign level by aiming beyond the object and the separation. Thought must tear away from itself if it wants to confront something which is not given in advance.

This tearing, for Bataille, can only occur in proximity to modified states of consciousness (drunkenness, voluptuousness, the sacred, interior experience, etc.) like for Sade ("philosophy lights its torch at the torch of the passions.") For Bataille, freedom is nothing if it is not the freedom to live at the limits where understanding erodes." (*The Impossible*). Baudrillard's regime of thought does not call for these limit-states that mix effervescence and anxiety. He is distanced, detached (from cultural, historical and philosophical problems), more ambivalent and more *cool*.

or the laborious accounting for the biases subjectivity introduces. Researchers are always guilty of inadequacy or subjectivity, subjected to truth, commanded to show proof and watched closely by their colleagues.[18] Researchers are like sinners, and truth is their God. Writers are only subject to themselves, their life, their visions, their violence and the rules they give themselves. This submission is, in the end, a greater cause of rigorousness than the objectivity that weighs on scientists. The submission to what provokes thought— but also artistic creation—this intellectual prematurity— controlled autism, revolt, revelation, tireless discipline to keep the mind free—presupposes spiritual asceticism. From asceticism emerges *style* and the author produces an identification for him or herself.[19]

Every work is first the mastery of a technique, a material, in this case writing. But it is above all the projection into the mastered material of what an author has found to express the beauty of life in its cruelty. Baudrillard's mode of thought is not only the invention of a singular topology in conjunction with masterful writing. Jean Baudrillard writes his own way of inhabiting the world, of diving "into the mental depths and metaphoric waters, into the murky universe of concepts."[20] In the radical approbation of life, every creator plays a sovereign game. It is from this excess of individuation, not the experience of ordinary alterity (*alteritas* in the sense of diversity), but radical alterity as a provocation (outside reason), that *seduction* becomes possible.

---

18. A "small world" described by David Lodge, Javier Marias and many others.

19. Maurice Merleau-Ponty wrote of Cézanne what one could write of any *necessary* work: "To be done, this work required this life."

20. *Cool Memories IV.*

The seductive alteration that a writer, poet or painter produces involves replacing reality submitted to *laws* with a *game* defined by *rules*. Not to share the game, but to exalt his or her solitude, offer us metamorphoses and make us more enigmatic to each other. In this way, the writer suggests an unmentionable community, a community based on something other than love—no one misses the others—but a community of seduction, of solitary people (those who do not have a community as Blanchot said). The expression of this interior experience, of this sovereignty creates the impassible boundary between programmed diversion, playfulness and festivities and the sovereign game. Without these forms of expression of radical acceptance "life would be an error," to extend Nietzsche's phrase on music.

— Marc Guillaume

# RADICAL ALTERITY

# 1

# Spectrality as the Ellipsis of the Other

**Marc Guillaume:** The first questions I would like to deal with are found in the figure that I have called the ellipsis of the Other. Simmel gave one of the most direct approaches to this theme in a brief text called *The Stranger* which I will only allude to in passing.

I will speak of alterity indirectly. It is something that is close to alterity but is not alterity. It could be summed up in the statement: taking the Other for others. Reducing the Other to others. Reducing the Other to others is a temptation made even more difficult to avoid in that absolute alterity is unthinkable and is therefore destined for reduction. In any case, alterity is always provocative. One example of this provocative thinking is a book by Maurice Debesse published in 1937. It deals with the crisis in juvenile originality, to use the author's own terms. The book is an example of how alterity is unthinkable. Adolescence is the moment when the subject refuses to be treated as an Other by others. The adolescent wants to be treated as an Other in his or her radical singularity. Isn't adolescence the moment when the subject must bury alterity? Maybe the parallel loss of the "wonderful child" that parents experience is the counterpoint to this teenage mourning. A teenager goes through the process of mourning alterity, resigning him or herself to being an Other among others. Parents also go through a process of mourning that Serge Leclaire described in *A Child Is Being Killed*, the moment when parents must kill the remainder that is inside them, the "wonderful child" that all adults leave behind with regret.

Without digressing into adolescence, one of the difficult aspects in thinking about it concerns radical alterity or the desire for radical alterity. Taking this desire into account would probably shed some light on the relationship between teenagers and drugs.

We are therefore naturally led, by a careless but common chain of associations, to use a distant other, for example a marginal or a stranger or some other that has a strong presence in our symbolic alphabet like a member of the opposite sex, as a hypostasis of the other. We cannot ignore this mental slide. It is baseless but deserves our attention.

Simmel's *The Stranger*, published in 1905, examines this hypostasis of alterity. For Simmel, a stranger is both near and far. "Far" does not necessarily mean a geographical or cultural distance; it means a boundary is crossed. The stranger's status is not like a judge or interested party, not someone who is partial in any debate or conflict or will remain permanently involved in our social surroundings. A stranger can therefore be an impartial observer, taking the distance needed to observe conflicts or situations that do not concern him or her in any lasting way. This distance gives strangers intimacy and places them in the position of mediators or even confessors. People confide in strangers more easily than to those closest to them. It is a remarkable relationship because the person farthest away also becomes the closest. This strange system of measurement shows that the relationship to the Other is twofold: both close and distant. A stranger is someone who, from one angle, is very distant and who, from another angle, is very close. The singularity of the stranger, this hypostasis of alterity analyzed by Simmel served as my point of reference when I examined a situation I call *artificial strangeness.*

Urban societies are populated with what we could call artificial strangers. There is an artificial production of strangeness. In this case, strangeness is not produced by the ellipsis of the Other but by the eclipse of the Other or, to use a more linguistic word, the elision of the Other. I will come back to the term elision in a moment.

A note on method before discussing artificial strangeness. My method consists of operating like an archeologist or paleontologist: finding the piece of rock or bone fragment from which we can reconstruct a reality. Paleontologists attempt to reconstruct entire animals from bits of skeleton. They recreate something that cannot be proven. Yet it corresponds to a supposed reality. In the same way, my attempts to reconstruct a social vision from a few symptoms may be used for prospection. You could also take it as an interpretation of the present, with the hope that the interpretation will seduce you. There are thus two levels in the reading of social symptoms. They can either be treated as a means to predict the future, and in that case it is better for the predictions to be good ones, in the utilitarian sense; or you can offer an interpretation of the present solely for your own pleasure. The only thing I hope is that this fragment will help us make strides in the analysis of alterity.

The fragment or symptom under investigation here is the proliferation of new forms of expression and communication that are made possible by technological devices and their industrial production and, most importantly, by a change in social sensibilities. The change in social sensibilities reflects the end of traditional communities, the weakening of intermediate institutions of socialization, the risks of anomie and solitude caused by sociotechnological potentialities that include the multiplication of urban connection networks and all of the "variable geometry" communication arrangements. In this sense, May '68 seems to be the last gasp of a bygone regime of sociality. It did not start a revolution; it ended one. People going out into the streets, joining nascent groups: the idea of an ephemeral but festive community was easily disarmed later by the media. Today, we are truly in a world of multiple networks giving rise to a new form of sociality that has nothing to do with the unrest of groups in fusion. This sociality can no longer be represented by traditional media and therefore cannot be disarmed or denounced by it as some elements of the traditional community once were. It is a form of communicability that causes us to break with the nostalgia of community, with the traditional dialectic of the individual and the community. I call this new mode of being and exchanging *spectral*.

Of course, isolated spectral behaviors are not new but the generalization of this mode is new. One can, sometimes at the expense of misinterpretation, find very old traces of spectrality. It can already be found in certain forms of communication like anonymous letters, graffiti, and in some forms of entertainment like carnivals, disguises, literary games, and some types of prostitution. In the 18th century, mask games and shadowy transgressions abounded. The same is true in literature. Stendhal juggled hundreds of pseudonyms, almost 300. Pessòa took refuge in at least three fictive personalities. Kierkegaard, Masoch, Borgès and many others including Julien Gracq and Eric Orsenna refused to be assigned a single name.

There is therefore a literary tradition of these games of simulated identity. But all of these situations are marginalized, condemned, forbidden activities or ritualized practices that serve as exorcisms against their potential generalization. They are even in some cases the behavior of a class or of personalities that wish to incarnate Balzac's saying: "going incognito is the privilege of princes."

In fact, the signs I have just mentioned may not be the origins of the current generalization. The generalization of this behavior appeared, somewhat ironically, where anomie seemed most present: through exchanges in cities that were called "inhuman," in crowds that were called "lonely." Where the worst was found, according to a Durkheimian approach to the social, a new society appeared. Specters who did not know each other crossed paths, specters who would never see each other again and yet still engaged in practices of exchange. Spectrality also spread in the attitudes of mass consumption. Mass consumption allowed a disconnection between social reality and social roles. It produced a space in which we learned to appear as we were not. It is something that has entered our daily lives but was unthinkable two generations ago, at least for ordinary people. Appearing as what one is not would have led to an uproar in traditional society. Today, everyone has gained the privilege of going incognito while the "princes"—at least those in the government—are kept firmly under the eyes of the people by the media and consigned to a certain transparency.

In cities, and through mass consumption, we have learned to manage a whirlwind of words and signs. We have learned to deal with incoherency, contradictory signs, and the "collages" of postmodernity. One of John Cage's phrases best characterizes this sensibility: "The world is a giant collage. A bus filled with people who don't know each other passing in front of a gothic church and a bright advertisement for cigarettes." In this empty space with its heteroclite directions, graffiti and tags, we learn to engage in spectral communication. We have to manage signs, manage roles and manage relationships with unfamiliar people, strangers with whom we have to share or make exchanges.

Leaving behind this somewhat impressionistic landscape, we can examine a more fragmentary situation that would allow us to grasp this spectral communication more analytically. Mediatized communications (instead of radio and television, think of the telephone and its offshoots) allow us to observe pure forms of spectrality in a context that is not very different from that of the city. The telephone and its avatars generalize the properties of urban accessibility and commutation. Commutation is what a city does: the capacity to establish contacts between people or between people and things. Cities are the locus of commerce, including the second, outdated meaning of the word "commerce." Urban connections are diverse: their intensity varies and they are sometimes weak or transitory; they offer the possibility to disconnect, to be alone.

Like a city, the network of communications offers a multiplicity of connections, the possibility to plug in or unplug. In this space for mediatized communication, spectral communication occurs when the agents of communication can, more or less partially and more or less provisionally, do without the procedures for control and identification normally required. They can escape, for example, from the identity defined or definable in traditional communication by names, prior recognition or physical presence. Ordinary communications are tightly controlled, channeled by their context and more generally by phenomena of metacommunication. All of these phenomena were catalogued and analyzed by the Palo Alto School with exemplary determination from Bateson to Watzlawik. They spent their time watching how hands moved, how legs were crossed, how cigarettes were lit, how affects were circulated.

In spectral communication, a portion of these meta-communicational phenomena are eliminated, set aside or suspended. Without any controlling authority or procedures for identification, this communication is private and disconnected from the cultural sedimentation of established conventions. It is communication destined for disconnection. As such, the work of the Palo Alto School hardly seems pertinent to these spectral situations. It only applies to ordinary communication. The forms of communication mediatized by technological artifacts have other controlling and contextualizing authorities.

Other codes will emerge but when, for example, one enters an anonymous procedure, the cornerstone of all former codes that were based on identity, identification, the nomen and therefore the nomos disappears.

To see what is new here, one must resist the temptation to picture spectral communication as partial, incomplete communication. What would be the Other, the absolute opposite of spectral communication? One might think it is the face to face, body to body between two people who know each other intimately, which we would then call a real, total communication. In fact, this is not the Other of the spectral because if everything is shared, if everything is common between two people, then there is no more communication. It disappears in extreme intimacy. It is a classic aporia: the aim of communication is the very thing that renders it unnecessary. In other words, all communication relies on its opposite and on the separation of beings. That is why communication thrives on all forms of distancing, strangeness, and all the risks of miscomprehension and misunderstanding. It is no surprise that technical progress, by removing communication from reality and spectralizing it, has made it more complex and more prolific, more existent. Spectral communication realizes the ideal of communication by intensifying separation. It leads us to seek a more precise answer to a conundrum: *the relationship between anonymity and anomie.*

How does anonymity come into play? The opposite of spectrality is totally identified communication and physical presence. Obviously, with a letter or by telephone, the body is absent but, in the case of a sociality that refuses anomie, the rituals of identification are rigorously respected and even patterned on face-to-face communication. Letters must have an identified addressee and a sender. There are rules, even quite strict ones, for polite expressions. The entire technical apparatus has been subjected to constraints based on cultural representations. The same is true of the telephone. It has been largely sterilized, diverted from many of its technological possibilities by the fact that it was experienced through a regressive imagination: everything must take place *as if* the people were face to face. One might say the telephone was aborted. The telephonic arrangement was only thinkable if it was seeped in good manners, if there was a servant to answer the phone and serve as an intermediary, if young women and even wives were kept away from an instrument that might lead to the eruption of nondomestic sociality. The telephone was thus castrated and then ritualized according to dominant social practices. The anonymity of the caller, for example, was strictly prohibited. Simultaneous communication between three people, which was possible from the start, was stifled. As often happens, a great number of technological possibilities were cast aside.

By contrast, books and newspapers introduced anonymity or rather unilateral anonymity since the receiver, in this case, was no longer identified. The anonymous, unknown and silent reader representing the masses and so-called public opinion—although this opinion is never published—took a new and important place in the field of social communication. In some cases, anonymity was even bilateral. If we consider books from the 16th and 17th centuries in France, and especially all of the critical thinkers (or the Protestants, who were published elsewhere under different names), we can see that this form of publication was a process exploring mass anonymity and establishes a double anonymity.

With radio, television and cinema, the unilateral form of communication became even more massive. In this situation, the sender seems well identified. But in reality, we only know the voice or the face of those in front of the camera or in the studio. They are also in a spectral position. These irradiating media hastened cultural change and the acceptance of very partial communication.

Over the past twenty years, technological possibilities that have not been diverted or sterilized have given rise to new practices or rather to a new status for old practices. The loss of identification that characterized the anonymous letter, graffiti or dazibaos has now ceased to be a marginal and exceptional situation or a morally condemned situation. In fact the opposite has occurred. Giving one's name has become prohibited. I am thinking of one of the first practices common to the Citizen Band. At first, the rule was that those who spoke would not give their name or address. The same was true for another, older use of the telephone "network" that started as a technical error but was then organized institutionally fifteen years ago by the directors of French Telecommunications in association with the city of Montpellier.

The CB and the telephone "network" were symptoms, without much consequence or importance, of something completely new in communication that abruptly occurred in French telematics. It is a situation where strangers talk calmly with strangers, confide in each other or invent roles and fictions in which anonymity is the rule. More precisely, heteronymy or pseudonymy are the rule rather than absolute anonymity. It is an example of convention replacing absolute anonymity with sometimes highly meaningful pseudonyms. Anonymity would then be defined by this new rule that would allow suspension of the old rules of ordinary civility. From this point of view, one could say that anonymity turns into a form of anomie because thanks to a type of eclipse, the ordinary rules of civility disappear. More generally speaking, this anonymity may create a rupture that separates the subject from his or her feeling of self and social context but also from reality. A break that promotes the liberation of the imagination and finally the admission of all fantasies—although maybe more to oneself than to others. Anonymity would thus be much more than a social operator: it would be a way to free the imagination and therefore to distance oneself from oneself.

It would be a mistake to reduce anonymity to this imaginary freedom. It is true that identification allows for more transgression; networks that make people invisible only reduce community social control, like traveling to the city from the country exposes you to less control. From this point of view, there is still an increase in urban commutation. Nevertheless, the search for anonymity or distance cannot be reduced to this situation. It is also a symbolic operator that allows the subject to separate worlds and to redistribute the worlds that he or she constantly confronts. It is a process of both separating and reconnecting.

For example, anonymity can be a way to recreate and introduce an identity. During social conflicts, in large national companies, employees used anonymous tracts distributed from workplace to workplace to express their demands. An anonymous concatenation led at first to the marginalization then the exclusion of the unions. Anonymity is a symbolic operator that allows one to create and inaugurate an empty space. Anonymity purges institutional excess and then, if the conditions are right, if the alchemy succeeds, it can bring about a new collective agent. By avoiding names before acting, by letting each person determine his or her self freely for themselves and for others, this movement let those left behind by the spokespeople and the hierarchies gain an identity and a collective project outside union norms and practices. The processes of creative anonymity are highly interesting.

More frequently, anonymity is the social operator that lets us articulate the social, utilitarian world—a partially inhuman world, both grandiose (the social, technological and economic world) and dismal—with the intimate, passionate human world, which is both pitiful and essential. Connecting these two worlds is a challenge every individual must face, especially since it is an impossible task: the two worlds are incommensurate. They are not just distant; there is no relation between them. We have grown accustomed to avoiding or overcoming this daily challenge. We use several types of "couriers" to face this challenge. There are the close friends and family with whom we discuss our problems in articulating the two worlds, but there are also strangers (in the role that Simmel discussed). Strangers can be a passing stranger or a "professional" stranger. A professional courier is typically a doctor or psychoanalyst, the "bureaucrats of alterity" as F. Perrier calls them.

Anonymity is also partially involved in our relations to doctors. The shifting geometry of anonymity here takes the form of doctor-patient privilege, a legally guaranteed secret that is also safeguarded by professional ethics. When we speak to a doctor, giving our name (although not necessarily), we can be almost certain that our name will be erased outside that particular encounter. Anonymity, which appears to be prohibited in our representations, is in fact organized and legitimized in certain situations when we deal with someone who might become a courier, someone who could help you cope with the incommensurability between the two worlds.

In some mediated communication, one meets random strangers who take on the courier role and who include themselves in the play of identity or the masks of identity and intersubjectivity. One example, on the most superficial level, is the possibility of exploring freedom of speech removed from all outside control, irresponsible speech that can switch between truth and lies, mixing reality and fiction. In this case, it is a very superficial game. It is not primarily an exploration of the Other but of the Other's roles. This dissimulation only ends in pure simulation: the "I" pretends to be an Other. Sexual transvestism is one example. Another example is electronic message boards. With the play of anonymity and pseudonyms, some users give themselves a socioprofessional or sexual status that they do not have. By choosing a name protected by the screen and texts, they can perform a kind of *textual transvestism* that they engage in comfortably and even innocently. Without the rituals of identification, relationships occur that are unthinkable in an ordinary and more rigid social context. *The elision of identity, like removing a letter at the end of a word, makes connections easier.*

However, it seems that this game of apparently superficial and inoffensive appearances can trick the subject, who in certain cases can be caught in his or her own truth. This speech, completely irresponsible in appearance, can cause the Other to emerge in the subject in the form of unconscious discourse. It is possible that this "idle talk, meaningless talk," this irresponsible speech is the maieutics of a discourse of the unconscious. An apparently pointless game could very well lead to the emergence of alterity, but an alterity that comes from the subject him or herself.

The social symptom described briefly here may not deserve much attention. At least, most observers see it as negligible. They treat it as an anomaly or a passing fad. There is a "ghetto" side to these social practices. Yet I believe that they are part of a more profound, mass movement, one with a development that we can trace through consumer habits and urban life. Spectrality is a mode of being that changes sensibilities, behavior and social relationships as a whole, beyond technical devices and beyond the uses of communication. In this general perspective, we can play on all of the meanings of the word "spectrality." The word "specter" has many echoes.

First, there is the echo of a disappearing, ghostly reality. Bodily presence starts to fade or lose consistency, causing a corresponding fear of transgression, dispersion, wandering, the loss of prohibitions, the rise of new exorcisms. It is also the echo of masks, doubles and multiples. From there, we pass into a new area of meaning: the spectrum of white light replacing an apparent unity with the dispersion of its component parts. This meaning is the richest. There is also a connection at the source between specter and spectrum: through appropriate optical experiments, (immaterial) virtual images are displayed with their colors dispersed.

Playing on these two areas of meaning with their various connotations, we could say, on the one hand, that phantoms—unreal or at least freed from that body and other procedures of identification—cause fear and therefore give rise to various exorcisms. On the other, the decomposition of an individual into several elements or facets, the possibility of connecting with others case by case, of having relationships of variable geometry, allows us to understand the idea of the courier, the idea of incommensurability mentioned above. Being spectral means having several faces and only using one in the communication interface, for example, in the ordinary social and professional world. One could show different facets to intimate acquaintances, family, friends and strangers. The restriction to a single identity can therefore be sidestepped and progressively eliminated. It represents a considerable social change that began in the mid-1970s. Two phenomena converged, at least in France, at that time: the ebb of representations exacerbated in 1968 or the end of mourning for traditional communities that would have recreated the village in the cities or the town in the country, according to traditional sociality, and the economic crisis that brought us back to the ideology of the "Post-War Boom," since the economic crisis was fundamentally the victory of the economy as ideology. When growth and its effects started to move out of reach, the masses began to play a double game. On one side, they played the game of economic competition wisely or intensely; on the other, without the dream of an impossible community, they invented a different sociality.

There was a kind of closure to the mourning over '68 and a regression to the past economic order. It led to the exploration for a new form of sociality. This new form meant finally accepting the dichotomy between the social and the intimate world within ourselves. This initial dichotomy can engender others, ad infinitum. By the same token, learning this double game establishes a multi-faceted spectrality.

The work of François Dubet on adolescents reveals a symptom of this spectrality. He showed that in some cases, especially in anomic situations, teenagers used to recreate communities in the form of gangs (the Black Jackets of the 1960s). Now, however, under the same conditions, no gangs are formed. Instead, there is something he calls "practices" that are difficult to name and identify and that do not lead to a new community. Dubet calls it "la galère" [struggle, hard times], using the same word as his interviewees. Their situation illustrates spectral practices.

There are in fact different levels of practices: teenagers use the adult world, urban references and, sometimes, social and educational assistance. At the same time, they invent transgressions, playing on all the different registers with ease, without trying to recreate an artificial unity. Their world is completely different than the world of gangs or even traditional networks like the mafia that recreate social relationships in reverse.

It is true that there are some gangs today—social reality is geological: strata accumulate on top of each other—but these gangs are not quite like those in the past. There is no exact comparison to past gangs because the gangs no longer concentrate all of these adolescents' sociality; gangs and galère can coexist.

In short, spectrality is not the destruction or disappearance of the subject. Spectrality is the dispersion of the subject. The same dispersion that Blanchot underlines in Foucault's work: "The subject does not disappear: the overly determined unity of the subject comes under question since interest and research are stimulated by ... a dispersion of the subject that does not annihilate it but gives us a plurality of positions and a discontinuity of functions" (in Foucault/Blanchot, Zone Books, 1987).

This dispersion opens one to the experience of the diversity (alteritas) of others, of the dust of often insignificant differences, but also to the experience of the diversity of internal components, including the unconscious component. Spectral exchanges with a multitude of others are not direct encounters with their alterity, although they might lead there in some cases. They contribute to sculpting the multiple facets of the self; they give rise to effects of alteration and alterity within the subject. They also produce a progressive change in sociality: we are no longer as much the products of our products, as Marx said, but the products of our virtual or real relationships. And therefore a plurality of positions, functions and interferences overtake the identified subject and disperse it. Bachelard once wrote: "Being does not illustrate relations, relations illuminate being." I would say instead that spectral relationships disperse being. Today's commutative sociality is based more on a generalized "relationism" than anomic individualism. It could even be the case that the excess of individualism or narcissism that people decry today is a compensation or a staging that helps the subject resist its dispersion, through the meditations in which it engages and that traverse it, to help it maintain an appearance of unity.

**Jean Baudrillard:** I like the word "spectral," but the two versions of it are not very compatible, even etymologically, because there is a ghostly spectrality (phantoms and ghosts) and a prismatic spectrality, the refraction of different colors from light or the different facets found in an "individual."

Ghostly spectrality relates to a disconnection: the ghost, the double behind the ghost, a very singular Other in the sense that he or she comes back to haunt you. That spectrality is haunted by emptiness and death.

When decanting the individual into different roles and facets, however, there is no haunting. On the contrary, the individual is no longer inhabited by something but is completely extrapolated, exterior. He or she is best described in terms of multiple connections.

No longer a ghost, the individual is in this case like a being with protrusions in every direction. There is a disconnection between the two meanings. And the disconnection is interesting. It means that it is probably not an element of explanation but an element of vision since visions can be contradictory and play on a *name* as long as it is a strong one. And the term "spectral" is very strong.

Let me add a few remarks concerning the ambiguity of the term "specter." There is no contradiction in your genealogy, moving from spectrality back to masks, carnivals and pseudonyms. Instead, you create an ambiguity. I wonder whether the play of appearances, the strategy that relies on the mask, is not a play on transparency or ghosts. It is a game with its own rules, not a real transgression. In modern terms, it would be called a transgression. Pseudonyms play on metamorphoses, not on ghosts. They do not rely on transparency or the loss of identity. The problem of identity is not even raised. The play of pseudonyms is a diffraction into networks of appearances. You cannot make it the first stage of spectrality. And then you make a jump and start talking about mass media. It might be better to speak of a mutation. You move from a local, intermittent and somewhat marginal phenomenon to a generalization. It is more of a direct mutation. It is hard to put the two together since they are not on the same register. One is in the register of symbolic operators: masks, the Other. And the second, as you said, is a simulation operator: playing at being an Other, pretending, which is not quite the same thing. In the play of appearances, someone becomes an Other with a certain awareness of the game. In diffraction or evaporation, however, the problem is: can one truly become an Other? As you say, one pretends. Is it still the same thing?

I also wonder what would define graffiti artists. They do not really operate in gangs. They usually work alone and are specifically interested in subways or surfaces and not at all in transgressive collectivity. Their goal is not subversion, but the simple play on the *name*. What they seek is not exactly anonymity, because they inscribe names and often their own name or code names. They are connected to the surface, the vector, the subway and only connected to the code, to code names, invented names that are completely destabilized and altered in appearance. The writing of graffiti itself is important and completely destabilizing. In fact, it is a wild game with the code. And they are less like aggressive gangs based on violence than a virus. Their actions are viral, atomic, atomized; they rely more on destabilization than direct confrontation. They play on anomalies more than anomy.

I agree with everything you said about spectrality. It seems like a very powerful vision and theoretical operator. I would, however, raise an objection about removing the name from bodily presence. Does it liberate us? Yes, we are liberated from all of the strong symbolic operators. But what kind of freedom is it? It is availability, virtuality, but we are still held hostage to the code.

When we are freed from our name, we become much more dependant on marks, signs, and all coded, referential signs. At that point, there is a precession of the code and ciphers. This is obvious every time we use the Minitel or the telephone. All of these types of media require a kind of preceding recognition through the code or indexed on the code, recognition preceding knowledge. You don't know yourself and do not really seek to know yourself.

The problem lies in the supremacy of the code. The code does not simply mean giving a code name for oneself. It is the technological matrix for the operation of those systems that govern the modes of appearance and disappearance, which is not the case of the pure linguistic operation with the name. The more one is removed from the body, identity or the name, the more one submits to the power of a frightening coding and overcoding. But this is not a moral judgment.

Sociality comes into play. It is no longer society. The suffix "-al" (society, sociality; virtue, virtuality; form, formality) is often ghostly. In relationship to society, sociality means we are no longer in the social. This communication is sociality, not a new form of society.

Does the Other exist there? If I pretend to be an Other at that point, the Other is also only an appearance, it comes from the code and may be part of the code. The great Other would be the code and there would be no Other. The code governs a perfectly artificial alterity.

I therefore object to the consequences of your hypothesis. It unfolds well, but in the history of anonymity and anomie, which you consider to be a positive distribution or a positive diffraction, is there not behind it all a great Other or another ghost called the code in which there is no longer any law or constraint? In a way, the code is unassailable because it is a matrix buried much deeper than the proper name. It is not a form, like the name, but a formula. It can be technological. The code is something other than a word. Take the genetic code, for example. With the genetic code, it is not a question of signing a contract. You do not communicate with your own code. It makes us communicate and it is there before everything; it comes before everything else. There is a precession of the code before all operations. Therefore, it is difficult to find the Other. On the other side of the code, there may be no more Other.

**Marc Guillaume:** It is true that the precession of the code could push interlocutors towards appearances or into having very stereotypical interactions. For a long time, people have faulted the artifices of communication for the poverty of the content of exchange. The code could even be very loaded when we are in the presence of the machines and devices of communication. We think we are talking with someone when in fact we "activate" a machine programmed to "respond" with more or less success depending on the talents of the programmer. In this case, there is a precession of the code (and of the programmer) and only a unilateral simulation of communication remains.

Outside of this extreme case, but staying close to it to some extent, if we combine appearances and stereotypes, we get pornography. It is not a necessary result. There is always the possibility that real writing, a challenge, an alterity will emerge from insignificance. Especially when the artifacts of communication make up a spectrum of tools from which we can choose. We can change the mode of communication at any moment, the exchange can become less spectral. With the Minitel, we have interactions based on a kind of writing that could potentially have a pornological feel (to use Deleuze's term) from which more real interactions might emerge.

These situations are similar to Masoch's approach (cf. Deleuze's preface to the reissuing of *Venus in Furs*). Masoch tried to explore the Other through a fictional literary situation using the limited technological means of his time: classified ads in newspapers, masks, darkrooms, etc. Masoch's Other is not only a woman, it is a unique hybrid because it carries the traces of its literary origins, the erotic charge given to it by Masoch's fictional imagination.

**Jean Baudrillard:** It may be possible to find our possibilities in language. Language is not a code, or not a formula-code but a form. This type of exchange is not communication because exchange in language calls into question its definition, its single-meaning. There is no internal paradox as there is in communication, where you say: the more we communicate, the more we destroy communication; or, the less we exchange, the more we have to communicate. The loss can only be repaired by more communication. And communication, with its self-referential, self-devouring circularity, ends when only the code or the network is left in operation.

You do not have the tetanic and somewhat metastatic enthusiasm for the symbolic use of language because there is a temporality of the to and fro, of the reversibility which means that there is not a total excrescence of the code and the network as communication. Communication is an infinite, tentacular, excrescent process that devours itself because it has no reversibility, because it cannot call the code as such into question. There is a limit that cannot be crossed: all of the communication that you mention moves through technological devices. Their formulas, their essences cannot be modified. Language by contrast is a form and one can play with forms. The same is true of masks and that is why I see a distinction between masks and spectrality. Whereas the technical prostheses on which all modern communication relies cannot be changed in their essence, in their very technicity.

You seem to be looking for the infraction in multiplication, speed, instantaneity, or infinite virtuality. In the end, it does not matter. It is merely the infinite reduction of the same. In other words, the medium comes first. But there may be possible infractions, transgressions of the code.

**Marc Guillaume:** I was looking for the infraction in the fact that, from the start, there is a kind of artificial strangeness. One speaks with someone who is a pure stranger. The artificial stranger encountered on a screen is Simmel's ideal type, someone who hardly exists for the Other and can still be turned into a confidant or even an accomplice. This operative coalescence can occur through (technical or social) codes that are like games, "coups" carried out in language, even if these coups are computer-assisted.

# 2

# The Other, Somewhere Else

**Marc Guillaume:** Let us now explore a form of exoticism called geographic exoticism. What is left of exoticism on a planet that, after offering very diverse, real or legendary models of alterity, now seems closed, incapable of producing an unknown, be it unknown lands or truly different social models? When the era of barbarians and savages came to an end, the Earth became round, voyages stopped and tourism began: the era of traveling in charted territory was born.

The transition from one era to the other gained speed and came to a close in the 18th century. The time of industrialization gave rise to the ideology of the scarcity of goods and, finally, the Other became scarce. Like all scarcity, it is betrayed by a contrary symptom: the taste for exoticism. The word "exoticism" itself was coined in the 19th century. Interest in the productions and customs of distant peoples existed long before that time, starting with the period of exploration, but the 19th century saw the first widespread expansion of exotic inspiration in literature and art. I see it as a terminal sign of the decline of the presence of the Other.

At this turning point, around 1900, Victor Segalen wrote a book on exoticism that is full of suffering. It is not even a book, just the outline of a book, a journal of sorts, a declaration of intent, a sketch, notes. It takes its source in his disgust with ordinary exoticism and his disdain for tourism and fake explorers. Segalen sees fake adventurers everywhere and tries to offer an original take on approaching the Other.

By starting our discussion of exoticism with Segalen, we follow in Jean Baudrillard's footsteps. I would even say that things have deteriorated since Segalen's first observations.

Our relationship to the Other, be it another country, race or sex, has completely changed. There are no more symbolic confrontations regulated by religion, rituals or taboos, for example. There is no longer a real threat of destruction: "If you are not like me, I will exclude you or kill you." Western societies have, on the contrary, reduced the reality of the Other through colonization and cultural assimilation. They therefore reduced the elements of radical heterogeneity or radical incommensurability that existed in the Other.

In a world of relative material abundance, we could say that there is a real scarcity of alterity. Perhaps the only way to fight this scarcity is to invent a *fiction of the Other*. Let me offer an example of this kind of oscillation between real scarcity and fictional compensation. The Marquis de Sade's work can serve as an example from fiction. When something becomes scarce, what does Sade do? He invents the sovereign hero, an absolute Other who in his solitude replaces and, since it is fiction after all, surpasses the sovereign of the Old Regime. The sovereign of the Old Regime was a man who possessed exorbitant rights by proxy because of his symbolic status. At least one could make that hypothesis. He also had sexual rights (as king or lord) that were exalted in Sade's fiction.

This idea—which is not mine—implies that at the moment when the real sovereign disappears, he is replaced by a being emerging from pure literary fiction. Of course, literary fiction has a great deal of freedom. It can explore without the weight of responsibility but it cannot support true exoticism without an object.

Surpassing scarcity through fiction is therefore a wrong direction, a dead end for creating exoticism. And one cannot fight the scarcity of the Other effectively without building what I call "combinatory fictions": something *constructed* from a certain reality and then given a dose of imagination and fiction. One source could be history, which is probably the greatest reservoir of exotic combinatory fictions. When objective alterity is gone, these combinatory fictions built out of the past could feed the need for exoticism through a kind of historical tourism.

Let us examine combinatory fictions from geographic sources in more detail. These fictions are constructed from what geography offers us in terms of the cultures and peoples on the planet. They exalt alterity and more precisely, they are specific to the ones who produce it. (In the same way, each new era builds the hybrid past that suits it from the traces of previous eras).

Using the reservoir represented by all of the different cultures is not easy. Its nature is also mixed. For example, you cannot invent a totally imaginary Morocco. Nor can you take an ethnographic position and develop precise descriptions of reality. What is interesting is to see how reality has been altered at different times in the search for alterity.

Most of the attempts that have been made, most of the travelogues now available are of little interest, except for those concerning Japan. I would even venture that Japan is distinct. But in my construction through a combinatory fiction, the Japan in question is neither an imaginary Japan—in which no one would be interested—nor the real Japan, which is inaccessible. The combinatory fiction is somewhere between the two. I am nonetheless obliged to hint at the type of epistemological question used as a starting point: something like the role of a psychoanalyst who cannot eliminate the patient's singularity and who cannot treat him or her without a minimum of scientific criteria. This is the "in-between" position I have in relation to Japan. I can only treat this country as a reservoir and will try to show it is unique in its malleability and its capacity to serve as an image that is truly in a relationship of alterity with us.

One might think that I am just following fashion since many people in many countries have produced texts—of varying quality—about Japan. Its social and economic organization, its technology, its history, its culture, and many other distinct aspects, which are more often appreciated by Westerners than in Japan proper, have fed a great number of fictions.

There is the specialist's Japan, the "Japan of the senses" to borrow Pierre Sansot's expression for France and all those who inhabit it. There are literary Japans, "ideogram Japans" like stereotyped blocks that serve as a model or counter-model, most notably for its economy and its social relations. But I will not approach it from this level, which is the ordinary reservoir that applies to any country.

There is more. The specificity of the Japan reservoir comes from this very surplus. The same type of fascination may have existed before for countries like the USSR, the United States and China, that were the stereotype of an upcoming revolution, an advancement to strive for or a model to follow. This fascination still remains with Japan and this general, lasting, compulsive and emotional fascination can be seen as an important symptom. If we know how to read and interpret this fascination, we might discover the hopes and anxieties of our civilization. And this leads us to a question that is implicit in everything we have discussed until now: What is alterity? Why do we need it?

I will try to show that there is a kind of core to what we are, something radically different lying behind the stereotypes. And by demonstrating it, I hope to determine how we construct it in a certain way. In other words, alterity is constructed more than it is discovered. It leads us down a path to the riddle: "What do we care about the Other?" Until now, there has been ordinary alterity and radical alterity. You may have wondered from the beginning why we are interested in others, what purpose it serves. We could have approached that question directly from a philosophical or psychoanalytical or other perspective but we did not. I hope that, in a heuristic manner, we will see that the object of our search has a certain structure. That is the goal.

Like chemists, we must therefore isolate the few consistent archetypes that combine to form the countless imaginary Japans that vary according to country, person, or point of view. Given the vast number of possible combinations, I will look for the basic elements, the carbon and oxygen that will lead us to all the molecules. I propose four archetypes. The first archetype is called the *apocalypse*. Japan draws on the archetype of the apocalypse for the simple reason that Japan sees its recent history as a new era of civilization, the era when nuclear holocaust is hovering at the edge of total annihilation: even though it is still a kind of fiction, the nuclear apocalypse became possible.

Hiroshima and Nagasaki symbolize a potential apocalypse for the entire planet. They also symbolize the possibility of surviving the nuclear threat and surviving under a permanent threat given the country's quick recovery after the catastrophe and the desire to memorialize the event to keep it from happening again. The threat reflects what Freud wrote at the end of *Civilization and its Discontents*: "Men today have pushed their mastery over the forces of nature so far that with their help, they can easily annihilate each other down to the last man. They know it and it explains much of their present unease, unhappiness, and worry."

After the observation that the earth is round, the observation here concerns temporal finitude. We can end our existence. This feeling of finitude also produces the scarcity of the Other. Just as the earth is round, it is also finite in time. Thus Japan represents the possibility of a transgression against this finitude, of living beyond, with the threat. The mixture of reality and projection, of our own anxieties over finiteness and our will to survive with the thought of this finitude form the first element of a combinatory fiction.

This vision of Japan sanctions apocalyptic thought or thought that foresees the apocalypse and considers going beyond it. For example, Jean-François Lyotard often speaks metaphorically about the four and a half billion years left for humanity because in (approximately) four and a half billion years, the Sun will explode. He states that this apocalyptic thought allows us to explore a certain metathought, since, necessarily, we are finite, if we want to survive, we have to think about going beyond our thought. He uses the example of the anthill destroyed by a passing foot.

Japan brings us more concretely closer to what Lyotard finds in the Sun and its finiteness. That is apocalyptic thought.

**Jean Baudrillard:** When Canetti analyzed the nuclear explosion in Hiroshima, he made the same comparison, saying that the disaster resulted from bringing the Sun to Earth. At that point, the bomb becomes the metaphor for this real, future event.

**Marc Guillaume:** Canetti provided the connection between Lyotard, Freud and Japan. He wrote that Hiroshima was the most concentrated disaster ever to strike human beings that was calculated and caused by other human beings. "Nature" is not to blame. Hiroshima is not Pompeii.

He added, about a doctor who kept a diary in the devastated city (from August 6 to September 30, 1945) and who was trying to survive and maintain the values of traditional Japan, that the Japanese people had never seemed so close, as if extreme despair allowed one to experience the Other as oneself.

The second component is *technological evasion*. The connection between technology and alterity comes once again through Freud. At the beginning of *Civilization and its Discontents*, Freud quotes the poet Grabbe who said, "Clearly we will never fall out of this world. If we are here, it is once and for all." And he sees this sadness and loneliness in the absence of another world as the source of religious feeling. Finiteness, the impossibility of leaving the world.

Alterity is basically the other way of thinking by refusing to think in terms of finiteness. Technology offers a way to fall out of the world, to think another world, to create an other-world simulacrum.

The technology of the 1960s, particularly as represented by the American dream, could be a symbol for today's Japan. It was, to use Eugénie Lemoine-Luccioni's words, "an astronaut's dream." It was the direct path out of the world by conquering the near-by suburb of outer space. But it was a relatively weak dream and only distracted the world from its finiteness for a short time.

What we can imagine about technological Japan at present opens a much broader perspective. Japan, in reality, has an advance over the rest of the world in its progress into cutting-edge technology, especially in information technology, the synthesis of the signs, communication and bioengineering. It produces artifacts, simulacra and automatons that give the illusion of circumventing reality and its constraints (time, space, the body). It appears to eliminate slowness, distance, and ultimately identity. In the end, it is a "rapture," an escape from the world, an escape from reality suggested in the escape from meaning. In particular, the development of artificial intelligence fascinates us and threatens to unveil, and therefore disenchant, the last *terra incognita* we have: the functioning of our brain and our thought.

The proximity of artificial intelligence to these remaining unknown worlds, however, is more imaginary than real. We have explored little of the way our heads work. We began with the unconscious, which allowed Freud to note a third humiliation (the subject is not the master of his or her house), but conscious thought remains a mystery.

Thus technological Japan represents a real astronaut's dream that both fascinates us and strengthens our fear of finitude. It is ambivalent: Japan shows that the world is finite and that it could be opened. The apocalypse is the presence of the end but we can survive it. Technological Japan extends Heidegger's question concerning technology: we not only question nature but we question humanity as well. Japan demonstrates this and at the same time suggests that, after all, it is not that bad and we can survive.

From this point of view, there is a Japanese strategy of acculturation that reveals its fascination with escape and stability, with human attachment to the world. An example would be the World's Fair that was held in Tsukuba. Its theme: the most futuristic technology is not opposed to nature, culture, or art; it continues them. One image that appeals to the Japanese and also to Westerners is the image of the *garden of accumulated technology,* a place where hope for the dialectical reversal called for by Heidegger can grow. A reversal where technology, in deploying its frenetic energy, reveals its own essence which is not very distant from art or poetry.

Tsukuba was Heidegger's dream of dialectical reversal incarnated and on display. It was a simulacrum of birds singing in the trees, or to caricature it, Heidegger's dream as seen through the eyes of Walt Disney. The world is finite, technology has questioned human kind and at the same time, we want to think that it is not so bad, that we can handle the inspection.

We now come to a more important subject and to Kojève, who will be our guide. Kojève dismayed French intellectuals of the 1930s with his reading of Hegel focused on the Hegelian end of history. Jean-Marie Besnier's book, *La Politique de l'impossible*, demonstrates the effects of this dismay on someone like Bataille while explaining Kojève's corrosive effect on the intelligentsia of the time.

When working for the OECD (the Organization for Economic Co-operation and Development), Kojève traveled to Japan on a mission in 1959. There, he underwent a conversion. He betrayed himself, and his betrayal took the form of a note published in the second edition of *Introduction to the Reading of Hegel*. The two-page note was the only one he added, giving it even more importance. If you publish a new edition of your book after fifteen years and only add one note, then everyone rushes to read the note. The first edition was published in 1939; the second in 1968.

The note is far from negligible. It expresses a kind of conversion or a betrayal of the despair he had professed for more than a decade. In fact, it is not exactly a note added to the text but a note prolonging a note already present. In the note, Kojève confirms the end of history in a brief summary of the despair mentioned above: "Several comparative trips to the United States and the USSR between '48 and '58 have left me with the impression that the

Americans appear to be rich Sino-Soviets because the Russians and Chinese are merely poor Americans, who are nonetheless rapidly becoming rich. I was led to conclude that the *American way of life* was the type of life appropriate to the posthistorical period with the current status of the United States in the world foreshadowing the eternal future of all humanity. Humanity's return to animality appeared less like a possibility yet to come than an already present certainty."

We can admit that ordinary people in American society or the Hegelian end of history, even if they do not recognize it, vaguely sense the fact that a functionalist, utilitarian world is a closed world, one that no longer solicits the specifically human trait of surpassing, of negating that which is. Thus the end of history provokes the dismay that Lyotard refers to in relation to a postmodernity that is merely the extension and not the surpassing of modernity.

From his position as a philosopher and his bureaucratic and economic observations in China, the USSR, and the USA, Kojève simply stated: "You see, the end of history is not only predictable, it is already here." And I think that corresponded to what ordinary people could already sense.

But then the note on the note becomes more interesting: "After a recent trip to Japan (1959) I had a radical change of opinion on this point. I saw a society that is unique in its way because it is the only one to have experienced almost three centuries of living in an end-of-history period, in the absence of any civil or exterior war. The lives of the Japanese nobles who stopped risking their lives, even in duels, without working, were nothing less than animal. The post-historical Japanese civilization is now following a path that is diametrically opposed to the American way. But *snobbism*, pure snobbism created disciplines that negated the natural or animal given, that were far more efficient than those that arise from historical action in Japan or anywhere else, which are revolutionary and armed struggles or forced labor. Of course the unequaled summits of specifically Japanese snobbery like Noh theater, the tea ceremony and the art of flower arranging are and remain the sole privilege of the rich and noble. But despite persistent economic and social inequality, all Japanese without exception are now able to live according to completely formalized values, emptied of any human content in the historical sense. Thus, each Japanese person could in principle commit, out of pure snobbism, a perfectly *gratuitous* suicide. The classic samurai sword could be replaced by an airplane or a torpedo, which has nothing to do, I would add, with risking one's life in a combat based on historical values with social and political content. This leads me to believe that the recent interaction started between Japan and the Western world will in the end lead to a Japanization of the West and Russia rather than a rebarbarization of the Japanese."

When Kojève wrote this passage in 1959, he was just discovering Japan and was still in shock so we should show some leniency when reading it. There are some lyrical passages, much exaggeration and it may make us smile. A Japanese person today could tell us that not all Japanese are ready to commit a perfectly gratuitous suicide out of pure snobbism. But this is one of the rules of the game. I said that we were in the realm of hybrid fiction and the same is true for Kojève. With Hegel in his head, he wanders through Japanese terrain and has a way of viewing Japan that is his own fiction: some reality but also the projection of his twenty-year anxiety. To paraphrase roughly what he said: can a world remain human and avoid becoming animal while accepting the end of history? Without exploring this end of the world's historical transformation? This part of the note becomes more complicated because it is very compact.

Can we imagine a world that finally goes beyond the end of history but remains human, a transhistorical world that stays human? At a more philosophical level, the problem is the same here as for technology and the apocalypse. Can we go beyond the apocalypse? Can we go beyond the questions of technology? Can we go beyond the end of history and still remain human?

Leaving aside the excessive or even comic aspects of Japan's sudden appearance in Kojève's work, we can see how he finds the hole, the possibility for survival in the term "snobbism." Personally, I would have used the word "dandyism" since Kojève's word can lead to confusion. Snobbism is commonly understood as a forwarding of subjectivity in its singularity. I think the Japanese formalism Kojève is referring to is more of an underidentification, a retreat of the subject into codes like the forms of politeness. The common meaning of "snobbism" is therefore inappropriate and unfortunate since it leads in the wrong direction. What Kojève is saying—and what Barthes will later use—is that the subject retreats into the rules of the game. The rules of the game come first.

With this precision concerning the word "snobbism," we can posit that the fascination with Hegel is also built on a double image of Japan. Once again, we encounter the aggravation of dead-ends and the possibility of going beyond them.

The first image is of a world that accompanies and even precedes the industrial West with surprising efficiency in its historical action of conquest and economic development. As such, and depending on the point of view, it appears as either a model to imitate or as an illustration of the limits and failures of society. At the same time— second image—it represents a world that follows its own secular path on a different and more or less cryptic level. This path includes the ideal of a formalism relieved of all content and even freed from the psychology of the subjects that follow it. This image inspired Barthes in his fiction of Japan. Barthes, at the beginning of the *Empire of Signs*, said that he experienced the realization that the structure of our society, especially in terms of signs, was not the only one possible and was not unsurpassable. He found that Japan allowed one to envisage a symbolic system that had nothing to do with what he called the Western semiocracy based on the imperialism of meaning. In an interview published in *The Grain of the Voice*, Barthes stated: "Like many of us, I deeply refuse my civilization, it is nauseating. This book expresses the absolute demand for the total alterity I now need."

The empire of signs for Barthes and for all of those who dream of escaping a world saturated with meanings finds its power in the emptiness of signs. It is basically a removal of subjective content in a world of pure formalism. All of Barthes's work as a literary critic comes from that perspective.

The fascination with formalism that inspired Barthes is the same fascination that inhabits most Japanesque practices when combined with the *American way of life*.

The possibility for difference would take the form of replacing reality with a rule, the rule of a game or of writing, which brings us closer to the realm of seduction. What fascinates Kojève, Barthes and many of us, even when we seem to be indulging in cheap exoticism, is a world *where the rule is preferred to reality*. Who cares if ordinary Japanese people do not commit suicide? What fascinates us is that ordinary Japanese people think it is possible. We do not think so because we never massively invented a world where everyone prefers the rule to reality. And the Japanese may still think a world is possible where everyone thinks: "I prefer the rules of the game, life on this earth based on rules, existence as a game (whose rules I might even be able to change) rather than leaving it up to the vagaries of historical evolution based on conquest." In this sense, it is a world of seduction.

**Jean Baudrillard:** Where is the seduction?

**Marc Guillaume:** Imagine a group of children who go into a corner and say, "Let's play!" You either accept it or you don't. If you agree to play, you are seduced. You replace reality with the game. Seducing means captivating, subordinating reality to formalism.

**Jean Baudrillard:** We could replace "reality" and "game" with two other words: law and rule. Perhaps seduction comes from no longer recognizing the authority of the law or from moving everything from the realm of law, or the reality principle, the economic, moral, political, historical, etc. principle to something arbitrary like the rule. The seduction is simply that we have gotten rid of the law, which happens with many other things, like games. But the fact that there is a transmutation that makes us pass to the other side of the law is a way of showing that it is possible to live as the image of the Other, somewhere other than in the law, on the other side.

**Marc Guillaume:** The added note displays clear ingenuity, like the echo of his joy in finding the way to survive beyond the apparent end of history. Kojève drove his listeners to dismay, especially Bataille who wrote him feverish letters and spoke of "things without us" to overcome his despair, "things" which were on the side of games rather than the law. Fifteen years later, Kojève passed through the looking glass of the law in these few lines.

I will conclude with a fourth stereotype, which is more concrete, called *interior alterity*, for lack of a better term. It combines elements rooted in daily practices.

A text by Oscar Wilde led me to this idea of interiority which is also connected with Japan. In *Intentions* (1891), Wilde wrote: "And so, if you desire to see a Japanese effect, you will not behave like a tourist and go to Tokio. On the contrary, you will stay at home and steep yourself in the work of certain Japanese artists, and then, when you have absorbed the spirit of their style, and caught their imaginative manner of vision, you will go some afternoon and sit in the Park or stroll down Piccadilly, and if you cannot see an absolutely Japanese effect there, you will not see it anywhere."

This passage echoes Chris Marker who said that alterity is not a problem of distance but the passing of a frontier, and a frontier can be totally imaginary and invisible.

It is true that the image of Japan in the West came through art, literature and, somewhat later, film. Through this image, characteristics appeared that gave access to, for example, differences in sexuality and eroticism or to several particularities unique to Japanese culture. They can produce a kind of minimal Oriental exoticism like the one found in Pierre Loti's work, which leads to superficial exoticism and sometimes to something more profound. As an example, there are the almost inordinate repercussions the works of Tanizaki and Mishima have had in the West.

Tanizaki, for example, provoked a representation by Henry Miller that is simplistic but also exemplary. In his preface to *The Key*, Miller wrote, "I have a mixed reaction to Japanese art and literature. Sometimes I feel like what I am reading is happening on another planet or talking about a newly-discovered species. And sometimes I have the same feeling I had with China, that everything is familiar, that what I see, hear and feel is the very expression of original man, the most human of all, the most universal of all the races on earth."

Japan is thus so far and so close in its literary fiction, as if it created a distortion in space. For the inordinate repercussions of some literary and cinematic works, I will use the example of Oshima's *Empire of the Senses* and the interesting analysis it inspired from Foucault.

The film ends with a scene that can be interpreted as a castration. For Foucault, it is not a castration at all and I believe he is correct since the man's penis belonged to both the woman and the man in the story; as an instrument of pleasure, it belonged to the woman more than to the man. The amputation of the penis is therefore not a castration, since it belonged to the woman more than to the man.

Foucault continues his remarks by making a major distinction between what he calls *scientia sexualis* and *ars erotica*. And he says that there is only one country—another example of Kojève's exaggeration—that has not reduced sex to a science, that still has an art of eroticism like there was in Western antiquity (which might also be imaginary). You can see how a projection of representations by a Westerner gives Japanese reality the effect of being both closer and farther away.

In the foreignness, in the fascination for a different or supposedly other eroticism, it is important to highlight the role played by formalism. You could find abundantly detailed descriptions of this formalism. One description of this extreme form of formalism is in the "flower and willow world," the world of the geishas, which is dedicated to the aesthetics of seduction and the dandyism of love. Guillan's recent book, *Les Geishas ou le monde des fleurs et des saules* [Geishas, the World of Flowers and Willows] describes the formalism of this eroticism in minute detail.

You can see to what extent everything contained in this art is primarily a snobbism in Kojève's sense, a pure formalism. The question is still important because the point of sexuality is the point of ordinary, massive, interpsychological alterity and is therefore the laboratory where we can see if the Japanese have succeeded in resolving the question of the Other in terms of sexuality, where all of the psychological problems could arise. Have they resolved it through formalism once again? This is an important point.

In this case, I am not talking about a real Japan but a laboratory that we can construct to analyze how the question of alterity is resolved.

A final point: when you import all of these exoticisms and esotericisms, you have a boundless source of fragments. We can construct different kinds of hybrid monsters using these fragments. Japanese society itself offers an appearance of proximity to the West under a thin film of Americanization that combines with everything and coats in the *American way of life*. Under this film, however, something else fundamental remains very distant and very closed.

There is something truly monstrous in the Japanese hybrid: an appearance of proximity and a core that rejects this proximity. It allows, often with deceptive indulgence, a direct exportation of cultural traits shorn of their context but with a foundation of universal snobbism that partially, superficially and sometimes grotesquely allows Kojève's prediction to take shape.

The imaginary Japan that surrounds us retains a common core that appears to be a utopia, a navel or an umbilical cord for all possible cultures; the part of all cultures that cannot be analyzed just as Freud said it was impossible to speak of the umbilicus of dreams because it resists any attempt at interpretation. This umbilicus might represent the pure exoticism that Segalen was looking for: "the acute and immediate perception of eternal incomprehensibility."

It is very close to Segalen, who wondered how he could avoid being caught up in the societies he encountered, how to avoid becoming Chinese in China. He noted that one effective method was to hate the Chinese, or not to live with them. He asked: "How do you keep your distance?" Thanks to the monsters listed above, the Japanese remain at a distance because an incommunicable core remains. And the proximity comes through the mediation of the Japanesque.

I therefore remain faithful to Segalen's proximity and distance approach since he said that true exoticism is based on a back and forth between recognizing the Other and returning to oneself.

A few concluding remarks. There is a point that has not been raised about Segalen until now. He clearly saw the problem of too much difference and in a way preceded and anticipated Marguerite Duras. In his *Essay on Exoticism*, he wrote, "Lovers would be horrified if they measured the unbreakable barrier that separates them even during strongest moments of shared passion, a barrier that will always divide them despite the apparent harmony of their unique joy." Marguerite Duras built her entire oeuvre around this kind of impossible community between lovers. And Segalen had already said it all.

He saw that too much difference makes the experience of alterity impossible. Only the back and forth movement provides some insight. Segalen warned us against superficial tourism and assimilation—the risk of too much proximity—but he also saw the risk that we would always be separated from the Other. He develops his thought on the impossible community by exploring the space between these two risks. His approach is therefore a *procedure*.

He was also fascinated by another approach that he called Bovarysm. The word has aged but I understand it as the idea that an individual creates a hybrid fiction using his or herself. This means developing a fictional being using his or herself, like in Flaubert's *Madame Bovary*. The real subject then appears as an Other for this fictional creature. Bovarysm is primarily an example of internal exoticism: I am caught in my own role and observe myself as an alterity; I create this distance inside myself.

Narcissism is an extreme case of Bovarysm. The subject creates an image that he or she ends up loving more than him or herself; the image kills the subject. Narcissism, as Clément Rosset remarked, often appears in people who do not like themselves enough. It is an illustration, on the internal level, of Segalen's approach to voyages as catastrophic. He saw voyages as artifacts that allow for an experience of alterity, a short-circuit that makes our attempts at alterity easier. We should add that the diversity of ancient times, of which Segalen regrets the decline, was not concretely or aesthetically perceptible. The world consisted of separate cultures that were relatively impermeable to exotic influences and there were hardly any "voyagers" to enjoy this diversity. This original exoticism is merely a virtual reconstruction.

Segalen's aestheticism appears strange: "Fundamentally, we need diversity, we need others because it pleases us, awakens our senses and the senses are life." We need to understand this sensualism. His response is aesthetic. He was passionate about paintings and he had a strategy of alterity in aesthetic pleasure. He did not want anything to do with the famous "correspondences" of the time—music relating to painting, etc. Segalen thought that music should be enjoyed in itself by separating all of the cultural elements. Taking pleasure in the aesthetic rule understood in its perfection and arbitrariness.

One of Segalen's contemporaries, with whom he is never associated, was Sacher-Masoch. In a certain way, he was another apostle of sensualism. Masoch also engaged in an experience of exoticism. He constructed an object and a procedure for relating to the object. To construct tyrannical women, he took real women and gave them fictive roles that both increased their distance and brought them closer to his fantasies.

I once used the emblem of the "Japanese woman" to represent my approach to Japan, as an echo to Godard's film *La Chinoise* (1967). The "Japanese woman" was also a way to increase the alterity of Japan through the opposite sex. I think Masoch fabricated his own "Japanese women": tyrannical women, artifacts of his own creation and a way to tame women. Why? For the sensuality, for pure aesthetic pleasure. Masoch's wild aesthetics is in the end close to Segalen. And Masoch's internal voyage is not very different from Segalen's exotic voyages in China or Tahiti.

**Jean Baudrillard:** My remarks will follow what you said about Japan since your analysis was very sound. In particular, it is important to circumvent the absolute misunderstandings that are so common with Japan despite the misunderstandings about mimeticism, imitation, the inability to create but great mimetic power. An absurdity that takes all of these forms.

The excursion into Japan might represent the ideal type of these allegorical voyages, a voyage that does not claim to capture reality. In the case of Japan in particular, for it would be a complete misinterpretation to look for reality in Japan if you want to use reality to grasp the game.

It is obvious that you must go there by going beyond this reality immediately, by passing into an allegorical projection, which is the best way to delve as far as possible into the knowledge of things while maintaining an allegorical distance from them. No mixing, no promiscuity is the secret of Japan and the secret of exoticism in general.

Japan fully poses the problem because there has been more confusion about mimetism and imitation in terms of this country than any other. For us, mimetism and imitation are values that are criticized because they are not authentic, original, or creative. So we condemn the entire system of Japanese values into a monstrous subsidiary of Westernness. And we continue to do it today.

The secret lies elsewhere, in snobbism. I will use your first analysis of the exacerbated state of technology and the resolution of technology by passing beyond it. Being more technological than technology leads to a kind of resolution of the principle of technology or the principle of technological reality. Japan goes beyond the reality of technology into a kind of hyperreality but also into an exterritoriality of technology that almost frees us from it.

Another way to see how it goes beyond is through snobbism. Personally, I think the analysis of the snob is very close to any analysis of the dandy. You said that the snob is more subjective. I disagree. A snob does not claim any universality and has no interiority in principle. For a snob, there is no psychological interiorization of values, signs, or forms; there is only affectation.

Affectation is the snob's quality. There is also a pejorative nuance concerning affectation in Heidegger's book. When taken literally, however, it is the sense of artifice of the artificial. There is no origin, no authenticity, no profound reality of things. Everything is formalized, seduced in the sense of being removed from its reality, its substance and its rules.

We can come back to the point that Japan might serve as an example to every other culture than ours, and maybe even to American culture. It would be a curious and paradoxical turn of events.

The fact that all of these cultures, unlike ours, are not "affected" by the virus of origins and authenticity. And Japan is not made for that virus. All of its writing and religion come from somewhere else; nothing comes from itself, from its being, its essence. That is our Western prejudice.

There, they recognize and take into account the fact that everything comes from somewhere else but that it is not really important. It is not borrowing but transferring things and enjoying the total freedom and much greater power that arise when the virus or the debt of the origin is absent. These cultures, and Japan most of all, are cultures of hospitality, not imitation. As though hospitality were given to anything that comes, including technology, capital, etc. It is snobbism in the sense that we have the impression that Japan is offering itself the luxury of technology, the luxury of modernity but a technology without deterritorialization.

For us, technology finds its reality principle in deconstructing territories. They can absorb anything because they are already on the other side. They can absorb the organless body of capitalism and the West without breaking their own secret codes, rules and rituals.

It is therefore something that lays no claim on universality in the Western sense but can accommodate, absorb and assimilate everything almost cannibalistically, transforming the appearance of everything. It is also seduction, the possibility of playing with signs, not in the universal sense but signs as signs. Barthes explained this phenomenon well in *The Empire of Signs*: the possibility of playing with and transforming the appearance of everything. Therein lies the secret of seduction and, in this sense, Japan made a wish that it can fulfill.

All primitive cultures act the same way. They integrate elements of Western culture like objects, signs and forms. They recycle them in their ritual circulation and cycles. Most of them do it out of desperation and poorly, because they are forced into it. But all cultures swallow the West in one way or another and there is something irreducible here that we are just starting to measure.

Japan is even more extraordinary because it has transformed the finest and most sophisticated product of Western culture: progress, technology, modernity. Japan is able to transform this technology and its essence and concept, capital, into pure strategy, games, and affectation.

Segalen spoke of this form of radical exoticism. We could try to look for it in primitive cultures with the idea that it may have resisted there. It is a much weaker form of resistance to say: "They are basically able to preserve themselves, there is a core that remains; however, this increasingly rare radical exoticism will one day be destroyed. Voyages are a desperate enterprise that will be lost." Segalen sometimes shared this vision and it is correct. Yet Japan is a counterexample because its radical exoticism was able to pass through the most crucial and determinant test of modernity and continue on after the test. It is truly something extraordinary.

The secret may lie in the fact that Japan has no illusions about its own authenticity, its own desire, or its own origins. With a fantastic modesty, it secretly thinks that everything comes from the outside, that nothing is proper to it, that there is no being in itself. This position gives them power over everything through its total flexibility. Fundamentally, the secret of alterity is to think that everything comes from the outside.

We in the West are doomed to think that everything comes from us and to feel guilty for it. Accepting responsibility for everything that happens to us is our ailment, our sad destiny, and the sad destiny of the West.

Can we talk about sexuality the way that you suggest? I am not sure. It is, however, obvious that, contrary to our own sexuality, their sexuality is not found in the realm of the proper, profound and authentic desire of an individual. It is more the demand to do it, to accomplish it. Perhaps the same principles apply to it and it also comes from the outside. Sexuality as an interiorized desire has an unhappy fate: repression. Alterity repressed within ourselves that we have not been able to treat or transform because it burdens us; there is confusion between us and us at that moment.

The principle of the Other has disappeared. Consequently, we have lost the possibility of keeping the Other as an Other, or the other sex as an other sex. In sexual liberation, we find ourselves involved in promiscuity. That does not mean it is nothing but that it is destined for a sad fate from the start because it is short-circuited by psychological interiority.

The same is not true of Japan, or at least of the model Japan we have constructed. There is the possibility that the Other remains the Other of the other sex. At that moment, sexuality appears to be less the accomplishment of a desire than a rite, a service, like the figure of the geisha who is much more distant and does not obstruct any exacerbated sexuality.

The distance from the Other remains. That is the principle of exoticism according to Segalen: keep your distance. Curiously, we would be tempted to enter the opposite form, which would be to go towards the Other, to assimilate or even play with difference to a certain degree and following a global and universal principle. That is the Other as Other. There is no universal, there is an Other, there is some Other. Keeping this situation is an impossible task for us because we are destined for the trials of interiority. Japan appears to be a fantastic example of this possibility. It seems—at least we can hope—indestructible.

After our detour through Japan, which is the strongest model, I think the same analysis can be used for every culture besides our own. It may even apply inside our culture. Kojève's distinction between Americans and Japanese in terms of their concept of things is true. But it may not be that simple and there may be something like an eternal incomprehensibility, as Segalen said, that includes our relationship to the American mode, as long as we do not take it as reality either. That is the problem. If we take the reality of things in an Americanized form, then the entire planet practically follows that form in terms of reality, in statistical terms. But that point of view is wrong.

**Marc Guillaume:** It is true that one can always find a point of view from which another culture appears incomprehensible, incommensurate to one's own. Japan does not have the monopoly on radical alterity in this respect. There are fictions of America, India, and North Africa among others that are just as enigmatic and captivating as the fictions of Japan.

But there are also times and spaces where these fictions become absolutely necessary and elicit extraordinary interest. At the end of the 18th century and the beginning of the 19th century in Europe, India and its language, culture, religions and philosophy exercised a fascination on British, French, and German intellectuals that has completely fallen off today. Between 1800 and 1810, there is even a veritable passion for India in Germany in the works of Herder and Schlegel that casts a considerable shadow through Schopenhauer and Nietzsche (for this subject, see Roger Pol-Droit, *L'Oubli de l'Inde* [India Forgotten], 1989).

On two different and more diverse levels, Japan has replaced India in the Western imagination. The current mania for Japan can be explained by fictions that have a specific point of view on a question with which the West is currently obsessed: the end of History. There is no need to look for a good angle to find Japanese singularity, since Japanese reality, with hardly any need for interpretation, seems to illustrate our anxieties and our obstacles. Hiroshima and the new technologies that question nature, life, and humanity themselves encircle our horizon and find echoes in our recent history (Auschwitz and the technology of extermination). Japan seems at first glance to provide a Western, postmodern answer to these Western questions and concerns (more postmodern than the postmodern, a kind of pastiche); it offers both a progressive and regressive world. The Tsukuba exhibition was a scale model of this world. But if we look closer at its response, we can see that the apparent response was only a polite answer. To a question forced on it (war, technology, capitalism and the questions they bring were imposed on Japan), a question not framed in terms of its culture, Japan answers, as is its habit, in the terms of the Other (and in a way better than the Other). But at the same time, it responds with artificiality and its own fiction, its affectation, which astonish us.

**Jean Baudrillard:** The root is *faire*, to do or make. In the root of *faire*, there is the artificial and the fictive is not too far either.

**Marc Guillaume:** I don't think affectation has the same root.

**Jean Baudrillard:** In any case, there are derivations that partake of the seduction of language; we cannot escape them, they are part of the seduction of language. The term affectation, if we reread it in these terms, renders the artificial or fictive quite well. There is in fact a possibility of getting away from the reality of things, from their meaning and their apocalypse. It is obvious that the linear principle of reality leads necessarily to an apocalypse at the end; there has to be an end. But a different principle, a principle of artificiality is something else. We can get out of it since even the apocalypse enters into it as an esoteric element. It would be interesting to develop this hypothesis since even affect is constructed—constructed in the sense of produced.

The apocalypse is the end of secrecy. Literally, it is the discovery, the revelation when everything is said. It is the end of metaphors and secrets. The nuclear bomb is the Sun cast on the Earth, or the end of the Sun as a metaphor, as distance. It is the Sun materialized on Earth: the end.

Let me return to one of the elements of snobbism since there is no correlation between signs and their meaning in snobbism. The snob—or the dandy—takes signs where he or she finds them; that is how snobs work and intensify signs. There is always a level of intensification that is almost a parody, an affectation. This is the problem of affectation: it implies an exacerbation but also a kind of liberation through the "more than," and not a catastrophe. There are no catastrophes in the "realm of the snobs." The rules of the game, of the game of signs, always come before real events. Even the apocalypse can enter into the general affectation, which is not particularly Japanese.

# 3

# The Sidereal Voyage

**Jean Baudrillard:** We are exploring the theme of alterity through voyages and exoticism but it is necessary to understand that we are talking about countries and cultures. This type of transversality or exploration is metaphorical. It is a way to "stroll" through the Other, the foreign, and to test its strangeness, to see if it disappears, if it is recreated or if it reinvents itself. The voyage, in the largest possible sense of the world, is a means or a possible scenario in this discovery.

We have made liberal use of Segalen and we can still refer to him. It is better to have a single reference than several different ones, as long as the reference is a strong one. And this one is strong. Segalen spoke of exoticism, which was his objective, his aim. He wrote about voyages that, "to receive the shock of exoticism—and therefore foreignness—it is not necessary to resort to the outdated episode of a voyage, but the episode and setting of the voyage, better than any other subterfuge, allow the brutal, quick and pitiless head to head confrontation and better record each of its blows."

The voyage is thus another type of ruse. But it is the best suited ruse of them all. It simply requires that one not lose sight of the fact that it is not an ethnographic trip or a picturesque tour. One must not be fooled by the voyage, the country, the daily life or the picturesque existence of things, which would lead to exoticism in the wrong sense of the word. "Not even by oneself," said Segalen. One cannot be fooled by a kind of identity or similarity with others. Such a game might be enthralling and very seductive but it is not the aim of this adventure.

For Segalen, and from my perspective, exoticism can be understood as a kind of fundamental law concerning the intensity of sensations, the exalting of the senses and life. The search it involves is much less defined. In Segalen's mind, it is a law. All men are subjected to the law of exoticism. There is a radical, fundamental foreignness that one must not try to eliminate in a general, picturesque fusion or confusion. The rule must be maintained.

Is the theory of exoticism that we are sketching here an ethics? An aesthetics? A philosophy? An art of living? A vision of the world? It is a little of all of these things. We see it as a curious and paradoxical hypothesis because it is fundamentally unavoidable. In principle, hypotheses are made to be disproved. This hypothesis, however, cannot be verified or disproved; it is a kind of destiny. In this sense, it is interesting, it is a source of pleasure because it is a source of seduction.

Beginning with the postulate that radical alterity cannot be found, reaching the goal is impossible from the start. That is why Marc Guillaume spoke of an impossible politics. In any case, finality is placed out of bounds. The search for the voyage, which is the metaphor for this, is also impossible. Segalen mentions this search: it is not an eternal truth; it is located in its time, its context. He writes that starting from the moment that the Earth was discovered to be a sphere and therefore closed on itself, it represented a kind of concentricness of things, which is the end of the voyage. There will never be another voyage in the finite sense of the term. There will be tourism, the idea of touring, of going around something, of circulation. But everything will start to turn on itself since, he says, as soon as you move away from one point on a sphere you move towards it in the same movement.

Linearity and infiniteness are no longer possible. There is only circularity within a "kitsch" form in tourism that covers the entire planet. As a search for exoticism, the voyage will have to take this circularity into account. We are no longer in the age of the great voyagers who thought they were discovering something and discovered it. At that time, there were stakes and also a result. There was adventure and the unknown.

Today, we know we are in an orbital world, a world closed on itself. We have to follow the law of its concentricness; we cannot escape it. At the same time, we must seek radical exoticism, like Segalen said. In orbality, we must seek a kind of exorbitation or exorbitality that could break the flatness of eternal tourism.

In fact, there is a paradox of voyages. I am thinking of the other voyage people speak of, a voyage through drugs. This kind of trip is not outside the realm of alterity.

What happens during this trip? Drugs are a voyage. But they are a psychodramatic voyage, a mental theater. As a voyage, drugs are not eccentric or exotic; they have no Other and are completely self-enclosed. They are an implosion of the voyage, an involution that traverses itself in an orbit reduced to the head, mind and body of the drug user. In reality, this voyage only thrives on its own alterations. There are no others, only a series of extreme and vital internal alterations or interior alterities that keep the subject from breaking out of his or her own life. There is an involution to that life and subjection to one's own psychodrama.

This is the end of the centripetal—and not centrifugal—voyage: the implosive journey that ends in itself in a single point, but a point from which in theory everything else is given to you. Being there is enough; everything takes place in the head and all cultures, visions and hallucinations are there, there is no need to move. The limit of the voyage is obviously here. It is also the limit of exoticism while at the same time its total contradiction and end.

In this dimension, in the metaphor of the ball or the Earth as a sphere, it is interesting that the more we explore its confines, the more we expand the circle of knowledge about different countries, the more the world shrinks. It is an inverse function: the more we extend the limits of knowledge, the farther we go in exploring the world, the more the world implodes and becomes orbital.

Segalen found that, like the drug trip, which is a total psycho-dramatic implosion, the Earth becomes smaller as we explore it more completely. The farther we push our discoveries, the more there is a kind of implosion that is the inverse destiny of exploration, the explosion.

Perhaps we could extend this image to another territory, the territory of the Other. We have all had problems communicating with others as human beings. Some have aptly stated that our true journey is the Other or others. In the end, the only voyage is the one made in relation to the Other, be it an individual or a culture. From this perspective, the more communication grows, the more we exchange with others, the more contacts and connections there are, the more we implode in on ourselves.

The subject of communication, if we can still speak of a subject, is a tiny point that governs all networks; it does this through the use of prostheses, obviously, screens and machines, and other technology. But at this point, it is a closed being, completely enclosed in its own screen and communicating with the entire world. The more communication becomes global, the more its epicenter is tribal, solipsistic and closed on itself.

The system of communication is dominated by a kind of paradox. There is a paradoxical law of communication, contrary to what one might believe, in the sense that with more communication and the multiplication of real exchanges, the exact opposite occurs.

For example, there could be an entirely communicative, imperative universe with atoms completely separated from each other, imploded in on each other. On the material scale of the planet, the more we explore the limits of the Earth, and as if by a kind of magic, the more it shrinks and becomes a kind of little ball. We must take this new dimension into account. It is an implosive dimension and certainly changes all of the laws, all the rules of the game, including our perceptions.

In his book *Us and Others*, which involves a voyage through literature, Todorov suggests a classification of travelers starting in the 19th century. After discussing Segalen, Chateaubriand and all of the great travelers, he lists ten categories of voyagers.

First, there is *the assimilator*. The assimilator travels to assimilate another culture, to convert it into reality. From Christian missionaries to contemporary Marxists, each traveler in this category is on an ideological, economic, or other mission. To a certain extent, colonists also seek a kind of assimilation or they are forced into assimilation out of necessity.

*The profiteer*. Profiteers are merchants. They travel without a relationship to the Other in his or her originality and authenticity. Profiteers are only the alibi of another law for the Other, the law of value, which is something else. They can be merchants and colonists as well since the categories can combine. But in principle, profiteers have no ideology to weigh them down. They travel, earn money, exploit, trade slaves.

*The tourist.* The third category is a complex one. Perhaps we will have the time to return to it. But we can have an image or intuition of it, even as a caricature since we have all participated in it at one time.

*The impressionist voyage.* This is the grand voyage of the 19th century, the one taken by Loti, Michaux and Barthes in Japan. During this voyage, intuition and sensibility or how one views a country play a greater role. Without saying that the subject is speaking, the voyager travels with his or her view of things. He or she does not claim to deduce any universal laws but enjoys the voyage. The traveler takes pleasure in difference and in that sense is impressionistic; he or she does not try to make things universal.

*The assimilated traveler.* As opposed to the assimilator, this voyager really penetrates a culture and adopts its way of life, like an immigrant. This voyager is no longer a voyager or quickly stops being one. The person may be an immigrant by force of circumstance or a voluntary immigrant but at some point, the question of the Other is no longer relevant because a kind of fusion occurs.

*The exote.* The exote is Segalen's traveler. Exotes keep their distance, they try to maintain the distance of foreignness while taking pleasure in difference. There is a strategy of delectation or seduction that leads to keeping a distance; one must not in this case try to enter, get mixed up with or lose one's identity. It is necessary to maintain a distance and develop tactics for this distance.

*The exile.* Exiles are another extreme of the voyage. They can include Descartes who lived almost his entire life outside France, notably in Holland.

Exile can be a charming situation or an unfortunate one (political or other exile). An important number of exiled writers, however, have found energy in distance, detachment and nostalgia, and have used it as creative inspiration. Take, for example,

Gombrowicz, who lived for twenty-five years in Buenos Aires. He set a standard for this type. Being deterritorialized in this way is a source of genius. If you do not lose yourself, therefore, you have a major advantage. To a certain extent, you have to be somewhere else to be truly alone. Which is another result of a strategy of exoticism.

*The allegorist.* Allegorists take foreign cultures and places as critical metaphors, they travel "metaphorically." They are never completely in the foreign country for itself; they are always in a critical relationship with their own culture. The other country serves as an allegory, a figure for forming a judgment and taking a distance from his or her own territoriality. Allegorists are intelligent voyagers but never decenter themselves. They remain centered in their own culture and keep their roots. They do not even exile themselves mentally but find a great complexity in their position.

One version of the allegorist is the disabused traveler who only travels to confirm the superiority of his or her culture over all others. Many French or American tourists only say one thing: how awful American culture is and no matter where they go they always see the same thing.

These tourists are to some extent excited to travel and discover new things but they do not play the game, they miss the exaltation of discovery. They only find a verification that home is the best place to be and that others really do have strange ways of doing things; that, in the end, the only real human beings are people like themselves. The topology of the disabused traveler is a centripetal discourse.

Todorov lists a final category, which he calls *the philosophical voyager.* His prototype is Montaigne. But this category is a bit idealistic. Philosophers are certainly universalists by trade. What interests them is difference in universality and they are not in principle ethnocentric. This is an ideal type and one might wonder whether it exists. It aims to have the philosopher verify the infinite variety and differentiation of values, cultures and attempt to reconcile them in a universal vision of things.

Like all classifications—we'll come back to the exote because that category interests us the most—this one relies on a blind spot. Classifications never reveal anything but serve as tools. They often forget to include the most important things or leave something out.

This classification may have left out the type of travel today, the voyage in its most contemporary form, for us. It is not exactly an earthly voyage but a stellar one, without mentioning space travel or flights in space. These voyages are pure vectors: simply a question of movement, speed and circulation.

An extreme case is the example of the woman (true story) who spent her whole life or long periods of her life traveling. She never left the airport. She went from one airport to another, boarded one airplane after another and traveled around the world. She even died in an airport! She was traveling, she was in orbit. This is the orbital, spatial voyage that is completely deteritorrialized even in relationship to the planet and it causes strong sensations.

Air travel, long flights are orbital. If you fly from Los Angeles to Sydney, you are in a little world; the flight itself is a destination. It is the world of entering orbit, where one even loses the idea of coming down in the end. There is the idea of no return, of going into definitive orbit following a vector that is now one of the specificities of the voyage.

Of course you cannot discover anything other than the abstract, formal universe of speed, space, and time. In the moment of the voyage, your concentration is focused on space-time in a dimension with a relative connection to things. This kind of voyage belongs to another context. It is more inhuman, and a little extraterrestrial. Its implications affect or contaminate all of the other types of voyages today. The reference for all other types of voyage may no longer be achieving a goal or getting to know people but displacement, pure and simple transfer-displacement.

Travel as machine-transfer: what is the Other of this kind of voyage, since we are still in the discourse of alterity?

There is no longer an Other, to be precise, but a kind of circulation or circumvolution since a long voyage always ends up circling the Earth in one way or another. The rhythm is no longer marked by discoveries or exchanges but by a kind of soft deterritorialization, a seduction through absence.

The voyage itself and therefore absence, which is also an absence to yourself, take charge. During the flight, you are in an airplane and you are no longer responsible for anything, including your own death. If death occurs, you have no responsibility at all, and this situation causes a very strong form of fascination, a secondary state that even translates into the body. Jet lag also causes a drugged, almost psychedelic state that could justify traveling in itself. Can we call it a voyage? I am not sure. It is an annihilation of your identity through longitude, latitude, altitude, and speed, none of which are dimensions traditionally sensed by the body. Bodies can get tired of this situation because they reach a point where they do not know where they are. An anamorphosis of the voyage occurs that is a distortion of the body but a delight for the mind.

In my view, this dimension is present in every voyage, even in the car trips you take to the coast. If you stay in your car on a highway for eight hours, it is the same thing as a flight, although on a smaller scale. It is a kind of orbiting that lasts as long as it lasts; it is a deterritorialization. And one pleasure we can look for today is a completely unfinalized pleasure. Your destination could leave you bored for a month and perhaps the only transfiguring, illuminating moment will have been the vector, the vectorial parenthesis on the way somewhere.

Our relationship to others today, which can be a psychological, social or other relationship, might come from this transitive, transversal, vectorial dimension. We may only be circulating in the desire of others, in the relationship to others. We can imagine a strong relationship to others with its own desire, a discovery of the Other, affect and everything that could constitute passion with some intensity. And we can also imagine the Other simply as a place of deterritorialization. In that case, the Other exists but is made to be traveled through; we can live in the Other's desire but it is like an exile, another dimension and fundamentally holographic. It is almost a hologram at that moment through which you can pass.

You are always traveling but there is no more resistance or any landings. There is a constant deterritorialization with an obvious need to pass from one territory to another because this type of voyage consumes its own space; it needs constant renewal. And here, one's own desire and energy count less than the desire to be taken in charge by transfer-machines or vectors.

One might also wonder whether others are in fact in a psychological relationship. At this level, there is no psychology. The Other is a formal space, still present but made to be traveled through like a kind of airspace.

I am not sure how far we can get using this hypothesis by analogy to understand contemporary sexual relations. This now sexual planet, this psychological planet, this psychodrama of the Other is not made up of desiring machines anymore like Deleuze said, but of circulation, of an almost empty space.

Once again, we encounter a fascination through absence. This absence is always on the move, it is not a contemplation of absence. It has to work, to travel. There is no stopping point.

One can finally bring back the same transparent memories from the relationship to the Other, the relation to others as from the voyage. Alterity, in this case, is like a game of absence. The Other would be like a metamorphosis, an anamorphosis of your own form. The other sex would also appear as an anamorphosis of the Other but not exactly in a strong duality.

The same can be found in the category of the allegorist. Allegorists see travel as a type of sport. They travel to rid themselves of their own culture. This is an essential point. It is hygienic to simply shed one's own culture, which may be quite rich and complex. It is yours but for that very reason, it is urgently necessary to distance yourself radically from it at some point. That may be the secret pleasure of a voyage, not in enrichment from others but simply in shedding your self, sloughing off a truly heavy weight.

Clearly, you can enjoy all of the positive aspects of your own culture, but you also absorb all of its stupidity; you are much more sensitive to it than in other cultures. So it always feels good to get away from your culture.

Imagine yourself in a desert in the United States. At that moment, the depth of European culture cannot come through, it evaporates, it vanishes; and this pleasure is part of the sensation of the desert itself. The sensation is spatial, physical, and, in some way, mental, in the sense that it is a radical evacuation of all of the heaviness, weight, and inertia of your own culture.

You can practice this anywhere, not only in the desert. You could experience it in a city or somewhere else, the main thing being that the place itself does not provide this radical foreignness but allows you to take in a minimum of estrangement from your own origins. I would say that it is an essential practice. It is something that what we can apply to Segalen in his concept of exoticism, one of the seductions of exoticism.

This form of expulsion and escape from oneself and from one's own desire is stronger today than the voyage of discovery or the classic voyage.

Why do we travel today? There is no more universal in the proper sense of the term. There is not exactly any possible synthesis of experience through traveling.

Of course, all of that continues to exist. It subsists even now in the aesthetic aspect of voyages, but these categories are less important than the ones that tend to make one's own culture reversible, to allow divestment, an escape from one's own space and one's own space-time. A voyage of escape that makes everything reversible or versatile or transparent.

It is the voyage of the Age of Aquarius; no longer a territorial or even planetary voyage but a versatile circumvolution that helps you escape the illusion of intimacy, privacy, identity, territoriality and everything that forms a very strong system of values but that is now severely called into question. Which leads us back to what we said about Japan.

Let us return to one of our categories, which we have been discussing from the beginning: the exote. This funny word is used by Segalen. We are going to see whether it still has a place, whether the exote, exoticism, the search for radical exoticism and foreignness is possible in this new dimension of the voyage, even though this new dimension is prototypical. In a way, it is behind all kinds of voyages and it constitutes, virtually, the dominant dimension corresponding to a passage into transparency, communication, the circulation of everything, the orbality of things and everything that relates to it, including sexual relations.

If the voyage falls into this orbit, can we keep the radical demand of exoticism that Segalen speaks of in the collimator?

I think so. We have already discussed Japan. We spoke of a transhistorical country subject to the transhistorical technology of circulation. And yet this country remains in the realm of the eternal incomprehensibility that Segalen mentioned. Now everything is changing, being modelized, evaporating but it remains an impenetrable mystery. And we are well obliged to think that even the Japanese themselves have nothing to say about it. They have been asked, but they cannot divulge the secret because there is nothing to divulge. There is just impenetrability, an incompatibility that, for Segalen, was an essential source of energy.

If this impenetrability and incomprehensibility end, if we are able to resolve all differences into a kind of universal plasma, the energy runs out, the charm disappears, the living stops. So it is good that it is the way it is and there is no need to seek out the neutralization of differences or neutralization through difference.

For Japan, we will draw no conclusions but we can still see that, even at the height of a technological, contemporary civilization, there is a kind of absolutely blind or empty core corresponding to what Barthes described as the "empty signifier." In Japanese civilization, there is always an underlying empty zone around which things are organized. We cannot decipher or interpret it, which is a good thing. We can of course find metaphors of this kind of exoticism in other countries.

Take Australia, for example, for the fabulous imaginary power of the antipodes. The Earth is a sphere but it nonetheless has two halves, and the antipode is not only a kind of opposite pole, but a completely different world. Does the difference come from culture, geography, or magnetism? No one knows, but you can feel it strongly.

The feeling is not as strong in Latin America. In Australia, besides the fact that it is a country where all of the flora and fauna are different, time is not the same, with an extraordinary slowness of things and animals that is not laziness. You have the extraordinary feeling of being at the antipode, a southern hemisphere that does not correspond to the same mental or gyroscopic laws.

The antipode is simply an effect of displacement. You pass a line, the Equator, which wants to be the line of equivalency and measure, but you find yourself in a world beyond equivalency, beyond correspondences and differences, beyond all of the things through which you can interpret a culture as different from your own, but that you can try to understand because difference is made to be understood.

Here, there is more than a difference. There is a kind of destabilizing power that is something else and that corresponds to the most intense phase of a voyage. And these grand voyages in space were the high period of travel in South America, and the high period of the Other when it broke into the world in its antipodal form, radically foreign, from beyond.

After that period, as we have said, there is the period of comprehension, recognition of the Other, exploration and domestication of this foreignness. But the moment of the eruption of alterity is the sublime moment. And for those who lived it, it must have occurred during the 18th century or perhaps a little sooner. Arriving in a new land is a moment now lost, but a moment that would have captured the joy of exotic travel as Segalen saw it.

That moment was a privileged moment. It was all downhill from there; we fell into the voyage. One could feel this foreignness everywhere. We saw it in Japan, we found it in Australia in a more naturalist form because it is inscribed in the geography of the antipode. We could find it in every country, including North America, the United States or even, I think, in our own culture. It is a distinct problem to know whether it is still possible to travel in one's culture like traveling in a strange new place.

I believe it is possible and that is where we depart from the ethnology we discussed at the beginning. Our approach here is the opposite of the ethnological enterprise. We are not trying to create a world of conciliation and recognition. In that case, on the contrary, one tends to return to one's own culture to reinvent it and explore its foreignness. We have the exact opposite stance: not reducing exoticism but inventing it, creating it or finding it if it still exists. This endeavor is at the opposite end of the spectrum from the social sciences.

I will add a few ideas about the United States. The same principle of the voyage, and not the voyage of recognition, can be found in going to seek the American dream, American life with its problems, contradictions and its real substance, the one we more or less know but is easily accessible.

I wanted to go there in a sidereal way. My first choice of a title was "Sidereal America," which means following a rule, keeping a distance. I am not addressing the reality of America; besides, what use is there in describing the reality of America since it is illustrated and described much better in American films and novels.

We must play with distance and foreignness like Segalen said. We have to accept this rule of the game, this illusive utopia of the emancipated. We will never be American just as we will never be

Bororo. You will never know the reality of a primitive society. Even the ethnologists who might claim to know it or who have sometimes tried to join in or merge with this strange reality are merely living a nice fantasy.

We have to keep this sidereal distance and not play the little game of difference and resemblance but try to see America—or anything else—as strange. At that moment, North America appears. It has been said that it is a part of our culture, despite its disproportionate size, that it is a stereoscopic magnification of European values and cultures. In my opinion, if you travel like that, America is a radically strange object completely distant from Europe.

It is a fiction. I will not say whether it is true or not but normally you construct a fiction of your voyage on a foundation of foreignness. Barthes did it with Japan. He said that he saw signs, signifiers that he could not understand. He assembled them and gave his vision of Japan in terms of something that completely escaped him but that carried the charm of a secret.

From this point of view, a country that appears close like North America but is radically foreign in its modernity will always escape us as Europeans. If you take it as a whole, North America looks like a mutant object. If you dig into its phenomenological details, you find that it is not. You can find many things and the voyage can become a game of discovery.

You can have the impression of transfiguration—which is a true impression—in deserts and towns, a feeling of mutation, of finding yourself suddenly in a new world, not only a transatlantic world but on another mental orbit. That is why I compared America to a primitive society. The Americans were not pleased. For me, calling it primitive meant giving it the most distance: a primitive society of the future, which also means something in terms of the truth that escapes us. The intensity comes from the fantastic distance separating the two cultures. I think that the American order or orders, the American state of things is fantastically different from our own. And all of the people who travel with the illusion of solidarity, often with the condescending, disdainful air of the disabused traveler, miss the point. I cannot describe it to you; you have to experience it. But it is like traveling to a completely different planet.

In order to reach this sidereal point of view, this radical distance, you must also be able to abstract the origin. It is always the same thing. It is true of primitive states and it gives Japan, which does not have the virus of the origin, its foreignness. Because if you go looking for the origin or the cause, everything becomes familiar but it also loses its secret.

You have to keep origins at a distance. America allows this better than any other place because its origin is so close. Or we could say that primitive societies are fascinating because they are closer than we are to a kind of mythical origin. We could consider America to be the country in the world that is closest to its origins, if it has origins; but it does not have any because it has broken with its origins. It has no originality of its own, and that is what makes it so powerfully fascinating.

From another angle, we could say that this country creates a kind of surprise for us as Europeans because it is so close to its origins. It is only a few centuries old, which gives it a mental world entirely different from our own. We have millennia behind us, even if we know nothing about them.

There is a short circuit of the origin. The origin is either totally emptied, forgotten and does not exist, or it is so close that it is no longer an origin. In either case, the territoriality given by the origin disappears but not originality since this deterritorialization produces an originality, a geniality to a space that for the most part is absolutely insignificant.

The space of the American way of life, in terms of objects and signs can be seen as totally insignificant. But this insignificance is interesting precisely because it connects with the empty signifier that Barthes discussed in describing Japan. The American type of travel does not even take the force of signifiers but it is almost more surprising. It is very surprising for us because we are used to making things signify and giving them a destination. There, we are suddenly relieved of this burden—because giving things meaning is a very heavy obligation.

It also leaves a puzzle: how is it possible for things to make no sense? How can a country have no culture? The desert metaphor is the ecstatic denial of culture, territory, and landscape; it is not even a landscape. You find yourself unexpectedly weightless, in orbit, with a kind of total foreignness.

It is the opposite of Japan. We could say that one can project rich signification onto the empty signifier. Signs there are so carved in stone, so ritualized that they are heavy but in a way we cannot decipher.

The opposite is true for America. Everything is light, transparent, floating. There is no meaning and no need to look for it. Radical insignificance joins radical significance in a way that creates a world completely foreign to us.

Beyond a certain history and beyond political ideologies, this also means that everything plays out differently, on a stage that is designified in terms of values, a stage of specularization and the total assimilation of everything. It is also a passage at the limits of our knowledge. We have the elements for this passage but we still live in a dense culture that believes in meaning and value. Over there, the change has happened. There is a paradoxical reality: it says that all values are more or less realized there and have materialized pragmatically. This comes from the fact that you can find everything you need everywhere. There is no need to imagine anything because it is already there in an object.

This kind of utopia made real, this millennial prophecy immaterialized in emptiness, creates a passage that we do not know because we have not reached that type of modernity. We are in a poor little modernity, a petty bourgeois, 19th century modernity; we never entered a model of modernity alive.

Without developing this point further, I will say that my perspective is aimed at learning about these mysteries of America. I do not mean a mysterious America in the cinematographic sense but the mutational riddle of a country that, on the opposite horizon, has rejoined primitive societies or even the signifying mystery of Japan. I believe it applies in all contexts and all countries; this core is contrary to what we say, to what we experience in the intoxication of a deplorable universalization of things, an Americanization of all ways of life.

I think that is an illusion and I do not know how to decide between them. In a way, the illusion cannot exist. It is obvious both that heterogeneity is indescribable and that incomprehensibility is eternal. As Segalen said, this is the law of things.

It may seem to be a gratuitous statement. It is in fact a radical hypothesis about the world. And in the state of things, at a level of verification, it is also true. You can really experience it in any country. And you only begin to realize it after going through several countries. At first, in the first phase of travel, you are tempted by uniformization or the recognition of small differences. But little differences are never foreignness; in fact the more of this type of differences there are, the easier it is for you to get your bearings.

In the first phase of travel, therefore, you could easily be convinced of a kind of uniform globalization, which is a very common theory today. It is, in fact, proven by tourism in the fullest sense of the word. But after a while, and obviously some countries are richer than others, the trend reverses. Then you are struck by the radical foreignness of all the ways of life in relation to each other. Take Brazil as an example. It has often, justly, been called the country of great American capital. All of the current signs of the most foolish globalization are present in Brazil: paternalistic technological civilization, banks, television. Sao Paulo is a wonderful global example, even more extraordinary than Chicago or other cities. Nonetheless, Brazil contains a radical antagonism between (North) American technological culture, capitalist culture if we can still use that term, and a completely different culture.

A parallel extension of a wild anticulture coming from the Blacks, the Nordeste has now invaded all of the cities. Contrary to what one might believe, this culture is not retreating as the other progresses. It is growing faster than the other. And the debate or conflict lies between the two cultures. One may be technological but the anti-culture is still a culture. We could also speak of quaternary culture and wild anti-culture.

For now, the debate continues. One has the impression that there is a completely simulating, quaternary, capitalist, technological culture being developed and that it is being devoured as is grows. There is a cannibalistic aspect of Brazilian culture that comes from the Blacks.

Rational culture is devoured by another culture that expresses itself through dance, festivals that one could reject as the vestiges of an unevolved culture, which is not at all the case. It is a completely dynamic culture that is slowly devouring the other. In fact, no one knows which one is devouring the other. There is no comparable situation in our countries. There is moreover no political sphere in Brazil; it is a completely crazy and simulating world. But the game is not over. No one knows what will happen with an assemblage like this.

Something odd is happening, however, is terms of racism or ethnic and racial differences. As you know, we have not been able to solve this issue, since we live with the illusion of being able to reconcile racial differences through integration or assimilation. Our rational utopia, however, will obviously not succeed. The more we try to eliminate differences, the more the racial phenomenon occurs.

Something else is happening in Brazil. It happens through seduction. Races there seduce each other. They do not fight each other, but from one race to another the effects of seduction can lead to devouring or cannibalism.

In fact, the racial question is "resolved" even though clear economic and other differences remain. But these differences do not exist in the mentality there because the racial problem is lost in the countless degrees of mixing. The antagonism is resolved through a total mixing of races that removes the object of racial conflict. There are other conflicts related to it but they cannot continue in the same way.

Racism is not fought directly or ideologically—the country itself is a big mix of everything—but mixing is a pragmatic, wild solution. It is a sexual mixture but at its beginning lies an extraordinary fascination for Whites and for Blacks. And it is still a culture without a truly dominant economic sector. There is a rampant and constant fluctuation of ethnicities and races. And this flux creates a mixture, a unique entity known as Brazil that, outside and next to the profound misery that exists there, causes a feeling of pleasure and joy that you can hardly find anywhere else in the world. There is an energy and vitality in the mixing, profusion and seduction. The assemblage is not familiar to us; it is radically different from our vision of social realities.

We could extend this exercise to other countries. Heterogeneity and foreignness can be found everywhere if we follow the rule of disconnecting from traditional, common ways of traveling and from the ideology that is always imposed on us.

It is not quite antagonism and it is not difference, since difference is a relative order. It is a radical exoticism to which we can refer in Segalen's terms. It is always there really or virtually and it is the only fascinating thing. The other process of de-vitalization, de-differentiation and de-identification is not without interest. That is why I said that this new category of voyages was part of that order. It is interesting, but the only truly fascinating and seductive thing is the indescribableness of this force, of the antagonistic foreignness that can be found everywhere.

The countries of the extreme south—Argentina, South Africa, Australia—each have very different statutes and legislation but they are all racist countries where there was an extermination of aborigines. In Argentina, there is even more of this savagery today, although the Indians have been uprooted, than in North America where everything is acclimated and domesticated. Patagonia and Tierra del Fuego are desolate spaces that have preserved this savagery. They are not free of political control but the space still is; it escapes territorialization.

They are some of the only examples of these spaces today, along with Australia, although Australia is not quite the same thing. These parts of the world have always been the stuff of dreams. Patagonia is the place where the deserters, delinquents, and anarchists met; they all went to establish communities there. It is a kind of collection and sanctuary for all of the marginals in the world. And for that reason, it is fascinating.

There is a naturalist nostalgia in Lévi-Strauss based on a profound analysis of the evolution of all cultures. In some ways, Lévi-Strauss cannot be contested; his ideas are pretty. But it seems to me that his pessimistic vision has its limits. Maybe we can use Segalen to correct Lévi-Strauss?

I would not personally attack him for his pessimism because it seems lucid. It is in fact the most intelligent, critical, and sensible vision we can have of the fate of all of these cultures and, through them, of our own.

He could not say the same things about the United States as I did. He created a model of annihilation and the end of cultures. I think we have to go to the other side, to see, not what is reproduced, but another kind of energy that is on a different orbit, which is not a question of territory. Territory is lost; if we see it as a system of values and cultures then all territories are virtually lost.

But something else is happening. There is another game in this deterritorialized space, a game that includes heterogeneity. And it is obvious that Lévi-Strauss is not a participant.

4

# Artificial Stupidity or

# the Intelligence of Others

**Marc Guillaume:** The figure of alterity that we will examine in this session is the figure of the so-called *intelligent machines*, a specific category of the set of interactive machines.

As in our exploration of the fictive Japan created for Western needs, I will not discuss real machines even though I will often refer to the reality of their performances or what I claim to know about them. Intelligent machines as we imagine them are a pretext for picturing other beings. From this perspective, the performance of these machines interests me less than their status as *alterity artifacts*.

The question is not a new one. The talking heads built by some monks at the end of the Middle Ages—Abbot Mical in particular—and condemned by the religious hierarchy show how these artifacts unleash all kinds of fantasies and impulses, as is always the case when religious condemnation occurs. In the 18th century, not only do the heads of the automatons speak but their bodies move thanks to the talent of French engineer Vaucanson. During the same period and in the opposite direction, considering man to be no more than a machine is a strong current of thought defended in particular by La Mettrie, a doctor and philosopher who by some twist of fate was born in the same year as Vaucanson, 1709. La Mettrie's materialist vision, as he developed it in *The Human-Machine*, extends

Descartes's materialism in terms of animals (*Animal-Machines*) to human beings. This extension was scandalous at the time.

The existence of a break between humans and nonhumans—animals or machines—was not a new question. It returned with Darwin and his successors in the next century and discreetly continues to haunt some of the debate over artificial intelligence. Beyond the technical questions that interest computer scientists and neurobiologists, this debate introduces a new dimension by considering different levels of human intelligence. The object under consideration is difficult to grasp because it is hard to distance oneself from it and set up comparisons. Machines offer a convenient reference point and term of comparison. They represent a first access point to an understanding of human thought, which remains a relative *terra incognita*. Curiously, we know more about the unconscious than the conscious mind, or at least we have been more interested in the former than the latter. We commonly use the terms "memory," "intelligence," and others without much precision and we combine notions that should be distinct.

To introduce my observations, I will use this phrase from Jean Baudrillard: *there is only intelligence of the Other*. I thought I understood this phrase when encountering it for the first time. Then I hesitated between several meanings, stopped understanding but continued to think about and with it. Thinking without understanding may be the strength of human thought, which gains its particular power from its imperfections. Zen teaching harnesses this power: the Master says or does something incomprehensible to his disciples. "Imperfections" of this type will certainly limit the capabilities of machines. Their "intelligence" seems at first both simple and perfect. In this sense, they are a concrete representation of the most simple Other of human intelligence, the elementary level of alterity. Following the first step of Jean Baudrillard's injunction, we need an intelligence of this Other.

The term "artificial intelligence" and its themes appeared in 1950. The big machines built in America offered calculating speed and power that had seemed impossible a few years earlier. When they were introduced in Europe, we continued to call them *computers* even though they could operate with symbols and perform operations that were not mere calculation. The French did invent the word "*ordinateur*" later, a word that seems more appropriate and has a religious connotation (ordination) that the word's inventor explicitly acknowledged (Legrand, a literature professor at the Sorbonne). Then, as a joke or by metaphor and more seriously by some, the idea was floated that these computers were intelligent. Or at least that they would become intelligent through future progress.

For those who wanted to found a discipline or legitimate and finance ambitious research programs, artificial intelligence started out as a nice slogan. But the expression soon resonated in the collective imagination and derivative expressions like electronic brains and artificial brains soon spread. More than just a theme that immediately mobilized specialists in the field, artificial intelligence has continued to stoke the imagination for more than thirty years and continues to feed controversy and more or less serious speculations.

We can examine some of these speculations by playing on the words that the founders of artificial intelligence brought together. One of the more eminent founders, A.M. Turing, opened debate in his famous article on the question "Can Machines Think?" (*Mind*, 1950), moving from artifices to machines and from intelligence to thought. He also tried to reduce the question to a game of identification and imitation: which one is the human and which one is the machine? His experiment also included: which one is the man and which one the woman? Using only the identity of the answers between the machine and the Human subject in this (too) simple game, Turing concluded that humans and machines were indistinguishable and, through a completely unsubstantiated leap, claimed that machines can think. His own thought seems frozen by its satisfaction with their indiscernibility. His fascination may be explained by aspects of his personal life but we will not examine this secondary question.

The connections Turing suggested had the merit of underscoring the diversity and heterogeneity of human mental processes. Some of them can be carried out or simulated by a more or less complex machine, a machine that has already been built or one that we could design. Other processes seem to remain peculiar to human beings, outside the grasp of any device—at least for now. The line that separates these processes is as vague as the term intelligence, leaving the door open for all types of ambiguity. Artificial intelligence is an expression with variable meanings, capable of fitting any representation one might have of human intelligence.

It is also an expression that was created at the right time. Artificial intelligence could have been mentioned with the first calculators or the first chess-playing automaton built by the Spaniard L. Torres y Quevedo in 1914 (although the automaton was happy to finish a match with its king and rook against a human opponent who no longer had a king). The ability to calculate and more generally to memorize and apply formal rules is certainly a part of human intelligence. A premature birth would have doomed artificial intelligence to insignificance. And a later appearance of its themes would have been much more problematic. We know now, for example, that some operations, that we do without even "thinking" about them, are beyond the reach of the most powerful computers. We now have a better sense of the immense complexity of the brain and therefore of its functioning. We know very little about how it works except to say that it is radically different from most computers today. Despite all of this and even though the term "artificial intelligence" is now challenged by most specialists in the neurosciences and cognitive sciences, it is now part of our collective imagination. The expression therefore came at the right moment. What people believed at the time about the future of computers and what they thought they knew about the brain allowed for naïve hope and ambitious research programs. At the time, A.M. Turing, H.A. Simon, A. Newell and many others thought that computers of the future would be able to think and to help us think about thought. Some more prudent researchers saw the computer as a tool, a powerful tool, one that could help us think but lacking any real ability to understand or reach other cognitive states.

This initial distinction has remained until today. There are two meanings of artificial intelligence. The weaker, albeit operative sense covers all of the research that attempts to use machines to simulate certain operations of human or animal intelligence. The performance of these machines has become breathtakingly fast and powerful and they have changed the conditions of writing, reading, memorization, and communication. The nature of the computers, however, has not changed. They include intellectual mechanisms that we do not consider to be on the level of human or even animal intelligence. They perform important operations better than we do, but these operations are nonessential. These machines do not use any of the *artifices* of intelligence.

They are more like the "idiot savants" who can find a cube root in a few seconds but whose intelligence in anything else, including mathematics, is often minimal. A child prodigy like Z. Colburn

(1804–1840) could calculate $8^{16}$ easily at age eight but he lost his powers when he went to school to learn. None of these prodigies knew how to explain the mechanics of their performances—even G.P. Bidder who became a prominent engineer. They lacked the intelligence of their deformed intelligence. It seems clear that the mechanisms they used were not the same as those engaged by today's computers.

In its strong sense, artificial intelligence has other ambitions. The goal here is not to build smart machines but simple ones. The hope of creating intelligent machines in the near future was lost with the relative failure of major projects like Logic Theorist and General Problem Solver (abandoned in 1967). But research into "thought simulations" (to use an intentionally ambiguous term) has multiplied and many researchers (Schank, Abelson, Winograd, Weisenbaum, Mac Carty and others) have finally continued, more or less explicitly, the work and perspectives of the founders of this current of thought.

Without going too far into their research, we can say that they display a touching attachment to a simple and naïve representation of intelligence and the brain. Their representation comes from a computer model suggesting that intelligence and the brain relate like a program and a machine. This comparison should not come as a surprise: representations of the brain can only borrow from available technologies. We can trace the progression from hydraulic models to electrical models to cybernetic models. These models can be very useful for concrete applications and even for understanding some of our intellectual processes. But the originality of the computer paradigm is the determination its defenders have shown in trying to demonstrate how it can help us think about thought and grasp its specificity.

J.R. Searle clearly revealed the absurdity of their determination (especially in his article "Minds, Brains and Programs," 1980). I will give a synopsis of his argument in a brief apologue.

Take an individual whom we know does not understand some thing, for example Mandarin. We place him or her inside a computer and by means of a ruse we make him or her strictly apply the directives of a translation program that makes the computer "speak" or translate Mandarin. You would not say that the person in the computer has learned Mandarin. Even if he or she mastered all of the formula that he or she applied, then he or she would only simulate an understanding of Mandarin. The person could, at best, evaluate the grammatical correctness of a sentence but would have no access to its meaning.

Those who believe and want others to believe that a formal program can create thought employ a rhetorical strategy allowing them to move from a simulation of thought to thought itself through a series of metaphors and analogies. In the 18th century, people already tried to astound and mislead crowds using automatons. Von Kempelen's automaton, which was a good chess player, caused a stir throughout Europe. It was in fact controlled by a small-sized chess master hidden in the base of the chessboard. Two centuries later, the procedures and intentions have changed, but the same fascination remains as to the possible abolition of difference between humans and machines. There is no need now to hide a person in a computer for it to play chess well; but some researchers are still trying to reduce the status of human thought to formal performances.

This does not mean that human intelligence and thought are beyond the scope of a device that we could conceive today and maybe build tomorrow. But it does mean that the device must interact with the program it runs and interact with its environment;

it must act like an interface, like a *body* and also acquire some degree of autonomy, the ability to organize its own structure. The simplest form of learning, which is even available to a modest marine snail (*Aplysia*), requires a rearrangement of nerve connections. Most computers today remain far below the level of "intelligence" of this snail (H. Gardiner called this the computational paradox). Other attempts in the very different direction of neural networks (F. Varela) might offer the chance of better performances.

Confusion in this domain stems from the fact that computers *use* concepts without accessing their intelligence. A formal program is capable of classifying concepts and applying the appropriate operations to each category. However, to reach the intelligence of the concept, as the human brain and *senses* do, it is necessary to start with the concrete and progressively distinguish an abstraction from it. Seeing, in particular, precedes knowing and the formal operations it allows. For a computer to have this kind of abstract intelligence it would need the means to perceive concrete reality, which would come from the machine and not programs. In the apologue of the person hidden in the machine to apply its program, we quickly understand that the lack of understanding comes from a lack of access to concrete reality. If the person can translate Mandarin by performing a series of operations on signifiers, it does not mean that he or she understands the language. Understanding means access to the signified, which implies something different: a mental image, a sum of concrete, corporal experiences, and more.

The current intelligence of computers could be called abstract but not in the way human intelligence abstracts: it is abstract without abstraction, formal but without knowledge of forms. Its power comes from the absence of reality that also makes it weak. What can we say about the other dimensions of human intelligence and thought? Computers should not only learn but learn how to learn, think about their thinking (the aporia that is as old as philosophy), think about their physical entity—their "body"—as distinct from the rest of the world, and many other dimensions. They should reach the Cartesian "cogito" without forgetting that Descartes also said that the soul is easier to know than the body. They should learn intentionality, especially the intentionality of never being content with being what they are. They should be open to communication, language and symbolic orders other than the formal symbols of programs, which is a syntax without "conscience."

We could imagine artificial arrangements that would give themselves objectives, that would take some distance from themselves, simulating "self-consciousness," "artificial intentions," and even "artificial desires."

Yet while nothing prevents us from imagining these machines, there is no guarantee that devices with these properties of thought could ever really be built, even in the distant future. Nothing is less certain, given the vast gulf that still separates the neurosciences from cognitive sciences and from their formal applications.

In this light, "thinking machines" play the same role in the cognitive sciences as extraterrestrials do in astronomy. We can imagine them and think that they probably exist. But until a trace of their existence is found, it remains a hypothesis. Thinking machines must remain a hypothesis as well.

Even if the hypothesis is proven, the connection between these two terms—thinking and machine—will remain a problem. I see Searle as making a play on words when he asks at the end of his article: "Could a machine think?" and answers: yes, only a machine can think and our brain is precisely that kind of machine. It may be a metaphorical way to underline his central idea that artificial intelligence "has had little to tell us about thinking, since it has nothing to tell us about machines." He plays with the word machine in an ironic way through an artificial extension of its common meaning that parallels the reduction of the meaning of thinking and intelligence in the authors he criticizes. Taking the expression at its word would mean going without proof from a minimal materialism that no one disputes (every mental process has a material support, like the brain, and relies on particular physical processes) to a maximal materialism in which all thought is reduced to these physical processes.

The difference between the objectives of these two meanings of the expression is significant. We can see that the cognitivists want to avoid the "vitalist" mistake of establishing an absolute distinction between organic and inorganic. But the opposite mistake would be to make a premature claim that this distinction does not exist.

Henri Atlan is much more circumspect in stating that this break may exist; and that even if it does not exist at a certain level, it can or perhaps should be posited *a priori* at another level. "The models that allow us to speak of artificial intelligence imply, beyond metaphor and analogy, a stronger—and therefore more restrictive— postulate of rationality in nature than the principle of sufficient reason." Logically, there is no way to decide whether the principle of rationality "is a property of reality, independent of the way our cognitive faculties function or a projection of these faculties whose success defines islands of rationality in reality."

Even if there is no break in the continuity between machines and the brain at the level of reality or of a reality projected on it, the subject/object distinction can be preserved by posing an *a priori* symbolic break between what is called a machine and what is called a subject. Because the essence of the machine is to be a means to an end. How can we imagine or accept a world where subjects would only be means for other subjects who would themselves only be machines? How could we refuse a minor adjustment to the Cartesian cogito: "I think, therefore I must be"? In the end, machine and subject are not separated by their capabilities but by the arbitrariness of a symbolic rule.

We can therefore expect no radical reworking of our philosophy of the subject's being from progress in artificial intelligence despite its surprising technological advances. However, the imaginary representations produced by this progress are interesting variations on the eternal theme of the human subject's dereliction in the face of solitude and death.

Created not exclusively in biological ways, an artifact accorded cognitive faculties, an alterity of our creation, is like the embodiment of the Promethean myth. Yet the creator's role does not deliver us from the human condition. It would be even more interesting if our creature could attain immortality. That would mean that its being-in-the-world was radically different than ours. Generally speaking, it would be exciting—and maybe easier—to create another form of thinking. Then we could realize the dream of the extraterrestrial (or the astronaut, to use E. Lemoine-Luccioni's expression) without traveling through space. Then it would be possible to "fall out of our world," which Freud deemed impossible and placed at the origin of religious feeling (in *Civilization and its Discontents*). Science fiction has eagerly explored the same possibility from its beginnings.

In this wild dream, we must still make distinctions. What can we do with a *radical alterity*, a "machine that has no idea of humanity" (J. Baudrillard) and with which we could establish no complete communication? Exploring this question, Stanislaw Lem has one of his characters in *Solaris* say: "We do not need other worlds. We need mirrors. [...] One world, our world, is enough but we cannot accept it for what it is. We seek an ideal image of our own world: we go looking for a planet, a civilization superior to ours but developed on the model of our primitive past." In these dreams of machines, we are looking for an answer to the mysteries of alterity more than a new way of thinking. We would like to create an intelligence—neither too identical nor dissimilar—that would help us reflect on our specificity. What would remain unique for humans when machines absorb or at least simulate our intellectual processes? It would help us accept our destiny.

Fundamentally, those who think we will soon be ready to build these machines seek reassurance and their ideas are seductive because they are comforting. Thinking we are close to machines rids us of the burden of the soul, of Dasein. Building artificial intelligence comes from a therapeutic determination to eliminate human mortality rather than preserve a life. A weak, regressive fantasy of the machine capturing the human-object in its orbit. Yet this fantasy heightens the fascination with radical alterity and the "primordial Exoticism between subject and object" as Segalen would say.

Dreaming of a machine-subject capable of initiative and communication or imagining a bio-computer hybrid with organic microprocessors is another, more problematic way to involve the idea of an absolute, transhuman alterity.

For this reason, our fascination with artificial intelligence is an extension of our fascination with the transsexual and belongs to the general index of gender exoticism.

It is a fascination that we want to be fooled by; it is a scientific fantasy. The computer form is very different from the telematic form, although in the latter form the search for the Other passes through writing stratagems and screen maneuvers that allow for ambiguity with subjects and machines. The motivation of eroticism is the constant search for community despite the insurmountable wall separating two people even when they are brought together by an apparent harmony. The inhuman alterity of an intelligent device raises the stakes of sexual exoticism. With inhuman alterity, we have entered the era of constructed exoticism and artificial alterity. The real new worlds of the third millennium will not be found in space or in the suburbs of our planet but in the complete artificialization of our planet and ourselves.

Examining the relationship between intelligence and alterity brings us back to the expression we started with: *there is only intelligence of the Other*. To comment on this expression, I will distinguish between three types of intelligence, although the second is more of a simple interface.

—First there is the *intelligence of objects*: mathematical objects, physical objects, human beings (if treated as objects bereft of thought). The geography of this first type of intelligence is very diverse. It is a calculating intelligence (machines, idiot savants, artists…) and its sometimes comic effects result from the connection between the mechanical and the living; but it is also the intelligence of forms and vague sets. The scientific paradigm established its regimes of universal truth exclusively in this domain, including the social sciences whose epistemological status leaves no room for the subject as subject. It is also the privileged, even exclusive domain of so-called scholastic intelligence.

This type of intelligence leaves no remainder (the result is correct or wrong, performance criteria are defined). And it therefore has its limits.

—Then there is the intelligence of objects and of one's self, or taking subjectivity into account. This intelligence by definition loses the scientific quality. And it quickly runs up against the impossibility of thinking the self without the Other (see the analyses in *Being and Nothingness*) unless it uses the reductive figure of considering the Other to be similar to the self. It is a passing intelligence that cuts a path for psychology, psychiatry, philosophy, but produces nothing if it does not lead to the third type of intelligence.

—Intelligence of the world, the self and the Other is an open, borderless intelligence. Here the Other is understood to be partially irreducible to the self, eternally incomprehensible (Segalen), both radically different and similar, or supposed to be so. The Other is the source of the incomprehension that, instead of blocking thought, keeps it moving indefinitely, eliminating any hope of absolute knowledge. This intelligence of the Other should be understood as it is in the expression "intelligence with the enemy."

It is a limitless intelligence because it always leaves something behind: incomprehension.

# 5

# Artificiality and Seduction

**Jean Baudrillard:** With artificial intelligence and the alterity of machines, we are still faced with the same issue: alterity is in danger. It is a masterpiece in peril, an object lost or missing from our system, from the system of artificial intelligence and the system of communication in general.

The general idea is that every current system of communication relies on an operationality that consists in a detachment of artificiality. In other words, there is no longer exactly believing, wanting, being able, or knowing. All of these functions or categories of the subject or action are taken up in a model that consists of making believe, making want, making known that information is something made known, that communication is something made to believe or know.

It is not exactly manipulation, but everything is comprised in the operational. All of the categories, instead of being categories of action become categories of operation. Everything therefore moves into this artificiality. I use the term artificiality (*facticité*) because it implies the auxiliary "to make" (*faire*): the auxiliary comes before all of the categories; everything moves into artificiality.

It is a similar discussion to what we said about simulation but with a different approach. This artificiality is the operationality of making (something) happen: making happen, making want, making orgasm. The effect of this artificiality, in this kind of closed operation, is to make the circle of action close, using soft or hard technologies.

It rids everything of its negativity because it closes these actions. "Making happen" (*faire faire*) could be compared to plastic surgery for action. It is like a face: in plastic surgery, they take away everything negative in a face to make it ideal, in theory, with only positive, ideal traits. All of the alterity, negativity, contradiction and asymmetry are removed from the face. Everything related to character, action or expression is generally smoothed over in plastic surgery to produce an artificial model.

I am not making any moral judgments but this artificiality is obviously not innocent. In particular, for what concerns us most with alterity, the face is a plausible example. A living human face carries a type of alterity, a contradiction with itself. There is even a form of semiological action in facial traits that plastic surgery partially erases. And we can transpose this plastic surgery onto the genetic manipulation that eliminates negative gene traits and finds coherence models where none existed before. It is another way of removing alterity, removing anything that is not homogenous, erasing the heterogeneity and creating homogenous wholes.

The same is true for every type of plastic surgery, like the aesthetic surgery on nature or in green spaces where all negative traits are eliminated until only the ideal model remains. Everywhere, in fact, there is a modeling of wants, bodies, and sex. We could even imagine a zodiac surgery center where you could have a sign sculpted in your image! An institute that would homogenize your needs, your desires, your lifestyle and your sign. Zodiac signs are fatal in the sense that they escape you. In principle, a sign is something that you cannot change, something unpredictable, incompatible, almost the minimum destiny that remains for us in this life.

Signs should be susceptible to remodeling in someone's image. We know that even sexual difference is part of destiny, of fate, since it befalls us. And it could therefore be reduced one day, since it is already possible to choose or change sexes. The aim would be to remove every figure of alterity from fate and ensure that everything that is not negotiable, that could not be negotiable, becomes negotiable for the sake of a general redemption of forms and signs.

Which leads us to the following question: what escapes negotiation? The problem applies to alterity as well. Are we still capable of determining the things that make up alterity, that are part of a destiny or fatality and are not alienation? The Other as a psychological partner, but one who alters your life.

What can escape the system of artificiality and still form a discernible Other, maybe a secret Other but with alterity involved and something necessarily fated in this alterity?

I am obviously preoccupied with this question. We are not looking for a psychological Other or, as we have seen, a sociological Other, a psychodrama of sociality or of alterity. There is the dialectic between the self and the Other in terms of opposition, comprehension and reconciliation. Books by Todorov and Kristeva, for example, deal more with the sphere of alienation than alterity, which is something different.

Alienation is the universe of relationships, of the self becoming Other, of the dialectical relationship between the two and the resolution of differences in our current game or cult or culture of difference. Racism is also part of this problem.

It is stimulating and complex; it has been much discussed. But we have said much less about another alterity that is not psychological, sociological, or metaphysical, but the Other in its purest state, what Segalen called radical exoticism.

Does this alterity, this Other, this adversity still exist somewhere? It is more interesting to see what could oppose the "making happen," the artificiality that involves a more or less complete erasure of the alterity I mentioned above. There are several things to mention. The opposite of artificiality is definitely not naturalness. In that sense, rediscovering nature, a natural alterity or a spontaneous, natural identity is like a pious wish.

There is the problem of modeled systems or machines. No need to be a computer to take part in artificial intelligence. All machines and all models functioning today at every level are part of artificial intelligence

These machines, as we are increasingly aware, are vulnerable. This is also true of social machines. Luckily for us, there is neglect, blackouts, inertia and breakdowns. The interesting aspect of these anomalies, these nonoperational residues when artificiality does not work is that we find, indirectly, some aspect of alterity, of the fatality exorcised from the system. In a way, the accidents would have been machinated by the Other. Alterity is altered in this sense. It is a metaphor to say that the Other is the machine.

All of the accidents, breakdowns, slips, skids, madness—in the end, all of this systematicity—is our alterity. It is our Other to the extent that we ourselves have become machines. We have functionalized ourselves. Nothing that happens to us has the same negative meaning that it might have had in the rational system. The bad signs are turned into good signs; not everything is caught in the general artificiality. But this is the perspective of accidental alterity. There should be another, more positive perspective. There is one that we have already mentioned, in particular in regards to Japan. We could oppose pure artificiality and operational artificiality.

We could ultimately oppose civilization and seduction. Both play on signs but one plays on pure signs and the other plays on the manipulation of signs. With the terms we are using here, we could say that artificiality opposes affectation. Affectation is the quality of something that plays with artificiality, that plays with its own operation. We should also remove the negative connotations of the word affectation that come from our culture of sincerity. We are returning to its literal meaning. It is the quality of being able to play well in an operational system, so well that it discreetly changes it into a system of signs and illusion. Affectation lets signs be signs when others think they are handling substances and being. One can be operational without believing in the Western operational system of references. We said it about the Japanese. It means sending artificiality back to its artificialness. Through a double switchback, we undo the "making happen" with a "more than." The "making happen" of artificiality is radicalized by more, not less.

In its most common connotation, affectation means doing more or too much. Someone who affects something overdoes it. Behavior, text, language are given a surplus of signification, bringing artificiality back to its purest fate. When we overdo it, we exacerbate sign and signification. It is the same as seduction, where evil is pitted against evil. We escape artificiality by increasing artificialness and affectation.

A brief parenthesis. We have used Japan as a model of the Other. It is an alterity for us, a cultural system more subtle than our own and certainly more powerful, even in the operational system. In the end, those who use affectation are freed from the system's meaning and weight, its ideological burden, and therefore become more operational than those who act according to good reasons.

It is a kind of ruse. It is Japan's strategy today. Yet I think this affectation is now general. Even in our society, which is now becoming completely operational, everyone obeys the operational principle without believing in it. I think that incredulity, agnosticism, and profound indifference are widespread. It may be an illusion or a utopia, but I have the impression that the system functions relatively well on this foundation of profound nonacceptance of the operational system and the artificiality of things.

Everyone is a little agnostic, unwittingly. Not everyone is conscious of it. The great majority of people are not cynical, but everyone is a little bit cynical in the characteristic affectation of overdoing it.

We can explain this phenomenon through the mechanical momentum of the system, but it may not be the only cause. There is probably also the ruse, the fact that, in reality, a kind of affectation reigns. The stress, tension and performance anxiety of operationality today are all a mad affectation and much more amusing when considered this way. There is an operational snobbism that affects us all for the better. Through this affectation, we rise above artificiality. It is almost an aesthetic stage of operationality, delivering us to some extent from the "making happen."

Here we have one of the strategies for escaping artificiality. Affectation is a paradoxical strategy of response in its excess: you overdo it. There would also be a paradoxical response by default that would suggest doing less rather than more: *laisser-faire*. The corresponding strategy in this paroxysm of artificiality would be to oppose "making happen" with *laisser-faire* "letting happen." Instead of "making want," "letting want"; instead of "making know," "letting know."

In French, we can make the distinction. But in German, the auxiliary verb *lassen* can mean both: to make and to allow. The context usually allows you to distinguish between them, but it is the same verb. English is relatively similar to German, although not as distinct. There is a balancing act, a potential reversal between the two faces of "making happen" and "letting happen." The strategies, however, are not at all the same.

It is not a negative form of desisting, renouncing, defeat or voluntary alienation—I let happen, I let believe, I let pass.... This may have been the case in a moral of action or a voluntarist morality but it is more a strategy of release, an ironic investment in the Other to whom we give responsibility for our desires. We are no longer responsible for our beliefs, wants, or knowledge; we transfer or divert responsibility to the Other. It is a trick of desire or the will in the form of a diversion or a type of seduction. We should therefore see it as a strategy and not a lack or passivity. It should be included among the strategies of resistance or even among offensive strategies, as way of exercising seduction.

Sometimes letting something happen works better than direct will or action. It is probably more powerful and more subtle to let someone believe than to make someone believe. While the media have the belief that their techniques make people believe, these techniques are probably less effective than letting them believe.

There is a way of extrapolating one's own life and desire through the Other and thus finding an alterity, since the Other is truly involved. The Other is not involved as a separate, opposite term. I devolve my desire and will to the Other and he or she is involved in the process of alterity. And even if we do not find a destiny—it is not that strong—the Other becomes an agent of my own life because he or she is in the end the foundation of this operation. I no longer account for the operation of my life; I refer it to the Other, who takes charge.

Some cultures do this systematically on the symbolic level. Someone else always takes charge of your life. In a hierarchical order, you do not have responsibility for your own life. Everything is taken in charge, either by a subsequent Other or a previous life. Almost all cultures know that no one has his or her own desires or will, that it is a utopian illusion. They know that things function and function better through a system of transfers, metaphor, and devolution. The Other takes charge of your life and you can take charge of someone else's life.

Will circulates in this circuit, which has nothing to do with artificiality. There is a form of resolution of deep-set ambiguities connected to all of these functions. Wanting, capability, belief, knowledge are functions that would cause us to be in complete contradiction if we took them on ourselves since we would have to oppose them to others. Our relationship with the Other would then be a relationship of force. This is not true of the symbolic relationship connecting each to the Other through desire and will.

We can credit psychoanalysis—despite everything else—for coming close to this connection. Or at least psychoanalysis transcribed it into our culture. In the pure, nuclear form of transference, psychoanalysis does not weigh itself down with analytical metalanguage. It has a secret efficiency; it is the heart of analysis, if such a thing exists. Analysis takes a stand in cultural differences or the cycle of evolution and fate. It tends to bring everything back to a reappropriation of the Id by the Ego. This account can lead us, therefore, to let believe or let happen, to disavow responsibility and will and no longer be able to believe, for example, but only to believe in the person who believes. In other words, only exercising this function indirectly but connecting to something else.

We can be incapable of loving but love someone who loves or whom we think capable of loving. We can want nothing or no longer know what we want but believe in someone who wants or who can want what he or she wants. A kind of general derogation takes place, a general release where capability, want and knowledge are left to someone else. They are not abandoned but managed at a remove, which can be negative or positive.

Take for example the function of looking, of looking at images. If you think about it, we hardly ever look at images by ourselves. We never see anything in all of the screens, pictures, videos and reportages that has not already been seen, recorded, mediated, and reconstructed. In fact, we are unable to look; we can only look at things that have already been seen. The same disconnection occurs here as with action and "making happen." In "making look," the disconnection translates as déjà vu, something already seen.

We appoint machines to see for us just as we will delegate our decisions to computers. All of these functions, even the organic ones, are relayed by satellite.

This strategy, however, can have powerful, positive effects. In the case of making believe or letting believe, let us take the example of children. Adults make children believe that they are adults. And children end up believing it. Children let adults believe that they are adults and that they themselves are children.

The two strategies are not equal, but in symbolic terms it does not matter. Adult beliefs, or their making believe, are never guaranteed to succeed while children's beliefs always work. In fact, adults believe they are adults whereas children fundamentally do not believe they are children. They are obviously in an unstable position; they do not have the illusion, they do not consider themselves children, or only in part, but they escape the system of belief that adults impose from the bottom.

Children do not let themselves be alienated into the status of children that is imposed on them. In terms of symbolic strategies, the adult strategy is no stronger than the one the children use. And the children win. Children are children but do not believe it. They do not believe in childhood as a superior state. Adults believe adulthood is superior to childhood. In the symbolic order, those who think themselves superior are automatically inferior. There is a reversibility that always makes them subordinate. Childhood, because it does not believe childhood to be superior and legitimate is stronger in this sense. But it lets believe, it has the tricks and seduction of childhood.

The same is true of the masses. This analysis has already been done. But it is true that the masses, by their very position of being forbidden subjectivity, are protected from believing they are masses. They do not believe they are masses. Who would do the believing? There is no subject to believe in that sense.

No one in the mass can say that there is no mirror of the masses, which distinguishes it from the political classes whose members believe and profess to believe that they are political, intellectual, and other types of subjects. They might be cynical but they still believe in their excellence. And this cynicism will never equal the masses who let others believe that they are the superior, intellectual class.

It has prodigious effects, not always visible in action as the interventions of political classes concerning the masses, but in the reabsorption of this political will by the masses, the profound indifference of the masses, which is an unconsciously calculated indifference, which is to let believe that it is the mass and that others can manipulate it using reason and discourse.

Obviously, none of those manipulations work. Masses never believe in themselves. Thus there is always another possible effect that can turn someone who believes violently in him or herself into a charismatic leader or a dictator. But charismatic leaders or dictators do not capture beliefs and aspirations like politicians. Dictators capture the masses' profound indifference to their essence. The strategy of letting believe, letting happen translates into believing in the one who believes, not believing in oneself but in the one who believes.

There is an example in another register that also concerns believing in someone who believes, loving someone who loves or following someone who travels. Instead of moving by yourself, you follow someone who is moving. I would like to return to the example of the book *La Suite vénitienne/Please Follow Me* by Sophie Calle. It tells a beautiful tale in which Sophie started following people in the street without premeditation or hidden intentions; she was following just to see. There was no intention to penetrate a secret or see where someone was going; it was just following.

After following people for a while, she moved to the next level: she picked someone she was slightly acquainted with, whom she knew was leaving for Venice on vacation in a few days and then started following him for two weeks.

The work was difficult because she had to find him in Venice during the carnival period. She finally found him and followed him. She took pictures of him everywhere, without him realizing it. He was with his wife. Sophie followed him, lost him, found him again and followed him some more. It continued for a long time. She kept a journal that she published along with the pictures she had taken.

What was at stake? She followed him. It lasted two weeks. She contacted an agency to find out when he was returning and arranged to come back just before him in order to take one last photo at the Gare de Lyon. It was a very complex scenario which required patience, effort, devotion, and something like fate. And it did have something to do with fate. Sophie, for a circumscribed period of time, created a kind of fate. Not the fate that is in front of you, that inevitably awaits you, but something behind you.

She made herself into this man's shadow. He went and she followed. Where did he go? There is no need to say; it is not a secret, there is nothing to reveal. He went and she followed. She was also there as a delegate or a proxy. She did not have her own fate; she followed him. She became the Other's fate, the shadow of the Other.

Taking his photograph is very ambiguous: the fact that she is there following him is proof that he is not going anywhere. Doing this changes the direction or meaning of his travel. The meaning that he believes he has in the various directions he goes in is in fact hidden, secret; it is following behind him in Sophie. His hidden meaning, the secret of his travel is Sophie. He, of course, is totally unaware. Or at least he remained unaware for a long time. There were a few incidents in the end when he finally realized it and things turned bad. People do not like being followed.

This secret, this dispossession of meaning, direction and life line ends up being felt. It is true that when you follow someone, no matter what precautions you take, you must be very subtle because it is like being haunted, dispossessed or doubled: the person ends up sensing it. At some point, everyone turns around and sees what is happening. The same thing happened to Sophie. The man was obviously upset and it could have taken a bad turn since she was taking a risk as well.

In fact, she could have followed him anywhere and he could have led her anywhere, even into violence. She took a risk. The final, more humorous episode was also a risk. When she wanted to publish the book with pictures, he was unrecognizable but he knew about it since he knew she had been following him. He opposed publication of the book, saying he would have it stopped.

To publish the book, she had to return to Venice with a couple of friends and retake all of the pictures in the same spots. Not only did the man become an Other in the sense that she was following him—the absolute Other—but there had to be a second installment where he was not only followed but replaced by a double like in the movies. The book was then published.

This story gave rise to serious debate. It is easy to understand why when we see that the game was subtle, discreet and seductive, but also very dangerous. It involved a person's trail and no one lives in his or her trail. Like a shadow or a mirror image, it is crucial, existential. If your trail is taken, a great emptiness ensues; it can cause death or at least symbolic death.

Sophie does this when she walks behind him. She enters his trail but she leaves no trail. She devours his trail and therefore erases his existence. As he moves forward, she erases that existence following him. It is a surprising risk.

However, she had no existence or desire of her own. She had no hidden agenda, no amorous or sexual intentions. They were not part of the game. The man absolutely did not interest her. There was a conflict at the end but there was no vulgar connotation or destination for this story.

As a whole it is secret, somewhat like the Secret Service except that secret services have an aim. Here there is no aim, which makes it much more mysterious and, in the end, dramatic for the person followed when he or she realizes it. The risk for Sophie was very intense but without content. It was the pure intensity of a double life. It was not the unhealthy curiosity of the voyeur to discover the secret of another person's life. It was not voyeurism or perversity even though it bore some of the signs. It was not aimed at revealing the double life or hidden destination of the Other.

It was being his secret, which is not the same as something hidden. In fact, the Other had no double life. His double life was the trailing. Sophie became this man's other life for a time without his knowledge. Another rule of the game was to keep it secret or discreet. There is nothing more to say. There was no resolution, solution or conclusion. It was a pure scenario, a pure event with no meaning, origin, or end since it was all arbitrary. She began one day and ended two weeks later. In principle, it would have all disappeared without leaving a trace.

But during that time, there was a play with destiny, a fatal game. In this sense, the man became an intellectual or fatal eminence. She did not embody anything in particular, she erased herself. It is obviously an operation on her self requiring a great deal of work, sacrificing everything. For two weeks, she had to be completely dedicated to it, much more than in any intellectual work.

She emptied herself of her own "thing." For several reasons, she lived in disguise. It was all a ruse thus she became a ruse. It is a type of seduction. She caught the Other in the ruse that is always behind him and it erased his own life.

Alterity is the Other of this man. Yet this Other is not in psychological or sexual conflict with him. It is not alterity or alienation in the weak sense. It is pure alterity. She is the Other and he does not know it; she is his fate. And in a way, he is Sophie's Other too.

In order for there to be alterity, there must be some reversibility. Not the opposition of separate terms like me and another person but the fact that the two are in the same boat, with the same fate. They have an inseparable double life by the very fact that one is the trace of the other, one erases the other. Alterity, in the fatal sense of the word, implies an equal risk for each of the two. There is total reversibility even though one is shadow and the other is being. It does not matter; it is reversible. And in this sense, there is radical alterity as Segalen envisaged it, not psychological, intersubjective alienation or alterity, which is a tainted form of alterity.

I could explain this example more thoroughly. But it is nonetheless an example of the search for a different alterity that involves forcing the Other into foreignness and forcing the Other in that foreignness. It is by no means an attempt for psychological reconciliation through dialogue, negotiation of identity or other means. Not psychology but a mysterious way of entering the life of the Other; not like violating the Other but being their secret. The Other has a secret and Sophie is at one point the secret of the Other's life. It is an ambivalent secret: it can be good or bad. In this case, it could have taken a turn for the worse. The conclusion of the story is unimportant. The secret has no destination in that sense. It is more important for it to remain secret like an unconscious obsession.

Along the same lines, I would like to present something very different that has a fatal but completely impersonal form. It is closer to a viral form. A quote from Schnitzler's book *Beziehungen und Einsamkeiten* resumes it best. Schnitzler formulates the following hypothesis: "We may be able to represent the progress of infectious disease in the human body as the history of a germ species with its origins, apogee and decline. Its history resembles human history; the proportions differ but the idea is the same."

This microbial species lives in the blood, the lymphatic system, in the tissues of the human body. A person who appears infected to us is its landscape, its world. For these minute individuals, trying unconsciously and involuntarily to destroy their own world is the necessary meaning of their existence. Who knows whether or not the different individuals of the microbial species are like human individuals with various talents and intentions, whether or not there are ordinary and genius germs?

Could we then also imagine that humanity is a disease for some superior organism that we are unable to comprehend as a whole and in which humanity finds its condition, necessity, and the meaning of its existence? Trying to destroy this creature and having to destroy it as it develops just as the microbial species try to destroy human individuals who fall ill.

And couldn't we extend this reflection and wonder whether it is not the mission of the entire living community, germ or human, to destroy the world that surpasses it? For our mind is only able to capture descending movements, never ascending ones.

In this sense, it may be possible to interpret the history of humanity as an eternal struggle with the divine, which despite resistance is slowly, necessarily being destroyed by humanity. Following this line of thought, we can also suppose that the element that surpasses us seems divine or feels divine but is equally surpassed by an element greater than it and so on to infinity.

I do not know whether this is true but we are not looking for the truth here. The hypothesis, because it is a hypothesis, is dizzying. Just as in Sophie's story, with the germ species and the human species, one is the secret and the other is too, it lives inside with the same fate since it dies the same death. Yet its destiny is on the contrary to expand, to reach its apogee and therefore sign the death warrant for the universe it does not completely know and whose death it will share.

Between the two species, there is complete symbiosis and total incompatibility since their reciprocal destruction is ensured so long as they do not know each other. There is no intelligibility between humans and viruses. There is not only difference between them. We cannot say that humans are the Other of the microbes or that viruses are the Other of humans except in a metaphoric sense. They are not opposed. They do not confront each other but are caught up in the destructive succession of species. And no one can think this succession. The connection is predestined but neither humans nor bacteria can think it. And these connections, according to Schnitzler, continue infinitely since we can suppose that the virus is destined to destroy us and we are destined to destroy the universe around us, the divine... and we do not know if there are still more connections beyond our perception.

Radical alterity can be found here. We could say that the virus is an absolute Other. In its total inhumanity it is an absolute Other. An Other we know nothing about, which is not even different than us since difference is intelligible. The hidden form changes everything. It is close to Sophie's tale. Sophie is there, hidden, secret and surreptitiously she changes the other's entire existence.

The two examples are similar. There is no possible negotiation or reconciliation; it is Segalen's eternal incomprehensibility. And yet this species lives the same life and dies the same death.

I am reminded of the story of a certain worm that has a type of algae in its stomach that helps it digest everything it eats. The worm cannot live without the parasitical algae. The situation works until the worm decides to devour its algae, causing the worm to die. I do not know if it can digest the algae, since in principle it can only digest things using the algae.

There is a reciprocal implication in their fate. It is not a confrontation but an osmosis, a symbiosis. We could ask which one is the Other of the other but in this kind of symbiosis, with its distances and total incompatibility, there is a strong form of alterity.

A word, in closing, on primitive peoples, since the question is always raised whether primitive peoples are Others. This alterity or difference has been much debated. And in fact, they have now become Others in the sense that we have tried to understand them, even if only to exploit or evangelize them. They are Others because we try to understand them and they are not incompatible. Even though the lives of primitive peoples are extremely different than our own, they are Others; they are different but not distinct from us.

In a book on the Alacalufe, a tribe in southern Patagonia, I saw described how they lived a miserable, inconceivable life at the zero degree of culture for a long time. They no longer exist but it took four centuries for the Whites to exterminate them completely. Over the course of those four centuries, the Alacalufes did not learn a thing. They never negotiated with the Whites, never learned their language, never truly spoke with them and never traded. There was total incomprehensibility.

Whites appeared to them as strangers. At one point, they called themselves "Humans": it was the name they had given themselves, their own name. Then they called themselves Alacalufe, the name they had given to the Whites and the Whites used that name for them. They turned the name that they had given to the Whites around and used it to call themselves strangers in their own tongue. In the end, they were called Alacalufe, which means: "give me, give me, give me" because they had no existence in any language. They were called the "give me": they became beggars. First they were humans, then strangers, then beggars.

For four centuries, they never considered Whites to be others or different or even something to learn from; the Whites remained something completely foreign and they continued to think their singularity. They thought they were humans, that there were no other humans. The superior people do not say anything. They will not borrow any techniques, they will not learn anything. But they remained humans—there were no others.

For the Whites, the Alacalufe are Others even if, at first, they were animals. Some time later, with the civilizing, colonial ideologies, the Alacalufe became Others in the way we mean it now. For the Alacalufe, however, the Whites were never even Others.

The asymmetry here is interesting. There can be a relationship of alterity where the other is one's Other while one is not the other's Other. I can be someone else's Other while he or she is not an Other for me. These dissymmetrical relationships can be extremely tragic and for the Alacalufe, it was one of the most horrible exterminations in history because of the disparity in the relationship to the Other.

Because we are seeking a harder alterity, for people like the Alacalufe, who are totally singular, at least at first, there will never be any alterity in the psychological, Western, differential sense. There will always be total alterity, their alterity, their impenetrable secret. They died without learning anything, without respecting the other or speaking to the other—they died in fact without doing anything we call civilization.

**Marc Guillaume:** The first time I read *La Suite Vénitienne/Please Follow Me*, I thought it was a technique to allow a man to take on the role of the seducer, a role that was difficult for him. Like in the zodiac clinic you mentioned. It is relatively easy for a man to transform into a woman but to transform into a seducer is much more difficult. And it seemed that he took on this role during the two weeks—in appearance, one only follows women; it is rarer to follow men. Men usually follow women in the seduction game and here he is followed. It led me towards this hypothesis.

He is in the position of seduction, not only in terms of appearances, but also because he himself has become a rule of the game. There is a double effacement affecting both of them.

**Jean Baudrillard:** But he does not do anything.

**Marc Guillaume:** True, he is an involuntary seducer. But a woman putting on makeup does not do anything either in a certain way. She dissolves into a rule of the game and then is followed. Of course seductresses have at least a minimum of know-how.

**Jean Baudrillard:** I thought he was seduced, objectively seduced in a manifest process.

**Marc Guillaume:** That is what disturbs me.

**Jean Baudrillard:** By following him, she diverts him since she diverts what he thinks he is experiencing into an obscure consciousness. This diversion is the seduction.

**Marc Guillaume:** Yes, but you have to apply your reversibility principle. She puts him in the position of seducer without his knowledge, whether he likes it or not. The difference with a woman is that he is unaware and at the same time radically feminized.

**Jean Baudrillard:** For you the typical scenario is a man following a woman?

**Marc Guillaume:** The typical scenario of ordinary seduction is two people disappearing into a ritual order. Make-up is one symptom. You enter into a game where one person captures the other's gaze with no amorous or psychological relationship. There is a common dissolution in the ritual. Here, there is clearly a very different rule imposed at the beginning, but it is not shared. But after the rule is imposed, it seems to me that the man is in the position of the seducer.

**Jean Baudrillard:** I meant seduction as a form. There is nothing sexual or amorous; it is purely fatal. The Other escapes him or herself sometimes. By following the man, Sophie represents the fact that he thinks he is going somewhere but in fact, more profoundly, he does not know where he is going. She knows, and she translates it. She takes the meaning from the other's wanderings. Seduction is like that. It means diverting from a direction, from an end. And that is why he became so aggressive when he realized what was happening.

There are two questions: why did Sophie enter into a game like this one, do we need psychological reasons? I would say no but the question itself is uninteresting. And why does she do it on a fatal level with that scenario, a pure game? And why does he become so vindictively angry when he realizes it? His reaction is normal, there is no reason to object to it but we can wonder what causes it. What affected him so deeply that his reaction really could have led to murder?

**Marc Guillaume:** I wonder if women suffer from the fact that men are never seducers, that there is no reversibility, that men cannot wear masks? Rather than a primitive psychological reaction, it is a shared suffering by women that men never wear masks.

In make-up, I see masks. Japanese culture is the best example of how women's make-up in the past was truly a mask. With women as subjects abolished by the mask. The suffering of the mask monopoly was so strong that things reversed and men started wearing women's masks.

**Jean Baudrillard:** Men were then unmasked beings.

**Marc Guillaume:** The Japanese responded with a culture of transvestites who were first characters with masks. It becomes a game of infinite reflection since women then started to put on make-up like the men who made their faces like women.

In our Western culture, Sophie Calle's very artificial experiment would be: how can we give a man the seducer's mask? You set a rule. It is very artificial. But isn't it like that, this dedication tied to personal suffering: how can one follow a man? Following is the pleasure of seduction for a man, at least as I understand it. You decide that a woman is your destiny and you take on that destiny in total indifference to her physical or psychological being. Pure seduction means saying: "You will be her and I will follow you." Men have access to this experience but not women.

**Jean Baudrillard:** I don't know. You are bringing in sexual difference, which I had not put in play.

**Marc Guillaume:** It is not really a sexual difference. I say man-woman to simplify things. It is true that women wear more masks and men are more unmasked. It is like a niche of reversible alterity that is used in male-female roles and is a faint echo of seduction.

**Jean Baudrillard:** I agree about make-up. You could say that Sophie's trailing disguises the other's existence or that she doubles it. Make-up highlights things and gives color. Everyone has his or her own approach. Sophie verifies the most insignificant details doubled in her photos and the text she writes in the margins. Insignificance is doubled by meaning and a massive signification of which it is unaware. It is like make-up or a mask in that the intensification or stereoscoping of things gives him breadth and meaning. Not a meaning that can be decrypted or decorated but an intensity that he did not have.

Could the same experiment work in reverse? Could a man follow a woman following Sophie's scenario? It might not be as easy since it is not an innocent undertaking. I think it is fatal and in that sense not perverse at all. It is simply fatal. It is the art of putting fate into play, of engaging the complete absence of identity at the base of each and every one of us that is hardly ever revealed because we constantly overcompensate to play with identities. It succeeds in fact in removing the other's identity and in losing one's own identity, leading to this fatal stratosphere. It is a game in its purest form with no necessary psychological connotations. We could say that in this game, there is Sophie and what she is but more important is that she reaches something that surpasses herself. She had the genius to stage it and the artificiality of her approach must be noted. You can have the idea but it takes something else to put it into action. Maybe the perversion lies there. You can have this strange idea, maybe even write something about it but enacting it is prodigious. There is certainly an obsession or perversion involved that calls for psychological considerations. You probably can never eliminate perversion completely.

**Question from the audience:** Does she strip him of his identity? Does she flee him or x-ray him?

**Jean Baudrillard:** In principle, it could be anyone. To set up the operation, she needed some information about him but she ended up learning a lot about him. What she learned relates more to the anecdotal, less interesting side of the story. Most of the following took place during Carnival, which is amusing since there were masks everywhere. And Venice is the ideal city for it because it is a labyrinth of secrets where you have the impression that everyone is following someone. It is a very cultured place but its culture has lapsed into secret, its tracks erased. Another remarkable aspect of the story is that it portrayed Venice as a city where all meaning is lost, where all destinations are combined. The city spins around itself in labyrinthine spirals; once you enter it, you find yourself in the situation she provokes or recreates artificially in much greater detail.

**Marc Guillaume:** You might add that in that kind of labyrinth, the only way to avoid encounters is to follow someone carefully without losing sight of him or her. Otherwise, you might always run into the person, which is what happens to Sophie in the end.

Something troubles me in your analysis. You mentioned ways of preserving strains of alterity. You brought in the seduction strain and the discharge or dispensation strain. There is a slow movement between them. In the dispensation strain, in the *laisser-faire* or "letting happen," I relinquish my will to an Other who, because he or she receives it, gains a status of much more radical alterity. Between this strain and the theme of seduction, it seemed to me, before hearing you or reading you, that there were two separate worlds: the world of slavery or submission and the world of seduction, which could be analyzed in Hegelian terms. And here you do not make the distinction.

**Jean Baudrillard:** Is the master the Other of the slave or the slave the Other of the master? In a class, historical or relationship of forces context, they are certainly alienated and that is where thought bases itself as a system of alienation. But on the symbolic scale, it is no longer part of a scale of value that we recognize as historical, and is no longer true. They are in a position of mutual seduction or reversibility.

In a hierarchical society, for example, the caste member is not the Other of the pariah and the pariah is not the Other of the caste member. There is no psychological position of alterity since they are both, like in Schnitzler's example, implicated in a successive order of incompatible developments. There is no negotiation and therefore no alienation to surpass or transgress. The two "castes" are perfectly foreign to each other and yet absolutely complicit in the symbolic order, in the succession of phases which is more like an order of metamorphoses since lives play on previous lives. It is more like a cycle of metamorphoses than a phenomenon of alienation or alterity. It is not the question of the Other. It is a highly seductive question because there is a kind of reversibility. The two are completely incompatible but fundamentally reversible since there is an order of progression from one form to another.

It is like myths and metamorphoses. It is interesting to see that in all orders other than our own, it does not exist and there is inclusion whereas our Western order of values postulates potential conflict and opposition between the self and the Other. In practically every other culture, when you read that the Araras are Bororos, that there is a cycle in which Araras and Bororos are involved, where there are no separate identities. There is the becoming-Arara of the Bororos; neither is the other's Other. They are metaphoric forms, successors in a symbolic order that combines all creatures and in which there is a form of identity mixing, and of seduction. Like Schnitzler explained, there is both total symbiosis and total incompatibility. It functions differently.

Seduction is even involved in the master-slave story. There is no more will. Each delegates his or her fate to the other; the subsequent form can be its own subsequent form. And the next form is not an other, in the psychological sense of the term. It is a fate, which is very different.

In response to a question, I would like to clarify that when I say "fatal" it is not in the sense of a religious fatalism. For me, "fatal" means that there is a recognition of letting believe, letting exist, letting want; a recognition that everything that happens to you comes from an inhuman order. It comes completely from somewhere else. It never comes from your own desire or will, since we do not affect to possess them, but it is true that most cultures are based on that type of thing. If it is not based on properties of the self, on identity, on appropriation of the world, then we are in the *laisser-faire* or "letting happen" in the noblest sense of the word and not in the "making happen" or "wanting to happen." Our culture, of course, is on the order of "making happen" and "wanting to happen."

This aspect of our culture is one of the tragic elements of the current relationship with Islam. This relationship may be the only situation today where there is true incomprehensibility. The two orders are completely different. For us, the Other is unacceptable and for them, our order is unacceptable. It is not a problem of historical evolution moving towards their quiet acceptance of our order. There is something completely irreducible or insurmountable. Western political psychologies do not take it into account because they cannot understand it.

In letting believe, letting do and letting want, there is a form of affectation. It is not simple. It is less simple than wanting. It is an affectation. There is a science of artificiality, an art of snobbism that says: "I am nothing, I let things happen."

When you say: "I want to be a machine," it is a pure form of snobbery. It is pure affectation. Yet through this affectation, we can reach the secret of the reproduction of objects and things by letting the world of machines exist, by only adding a little to it. It is one more machine, a little machine that makes the artificiality of all the other machines. Once again we are in the "little bit more." It is the oversignification that we always bring to something. But we let it come; we do not claim to invent or change the world or even to interpret it and give it meaning. There is a great affectation in relinquishing yourself to the obviousness of the world, to the pure metabolic of things, to pure events or to the other's will.

Masses are similar. Everything happens as if they deferred to someone else—the media or politicians—and gave them the responsibility for interpreting everything. Masses do not interpret. They have no intelligence. They do not seek to understand. They let others interpret and desire for them. It is an extraordinary affectation.

Snobs do the same thing; they do not have their own will. It is like Brummel: "Tell me what I like." There is the story of his exchange with his valet in Scotland before the lakes. He turns to his valet and asks: "Which lake do I prefer?" He has no need for his own desires. He does not exist. That is affectation.

For us, this process has a negative connotation and given a completely pejorative value. It is a passive strategy. I do not want to make connections with Eastern philosophies. We can talk about Japan but Japan today. Otherwise, you could find infinite connections to these philosophies which are philosophies of *laisser-faire* and reversibility.

**Marc Guillaume:** The break with seduction and reversibility is radical in comparison to Hegel's work. If you reread the first pages of Kojève's introduction to his reading of Hegel, you will see that they posit the axiom of the necessity of putting oneself in the position of being the other's object of desire in order for the human subject to appear. There is an entire dialectic from which the idea of passivity and reversibility are excluded. It is like the birth of another axiomatic system. All of the analyses that followed accept, at least partially, this Hegelian axiom. The notion of seduction and the reversibility it introduces are therefore something like changing geometries.

**Jean Baudrillard:** Yes, it leads out of alienation, and completely out of all of the greatness and decadence of alienation.

**Question from the audience:** Extending the question of activity and passivity, don't you think there is a gap between a book and an experience? When Sophie Calle records her shadowing with language, she goes beyond the mute experience where there is a reversibility in the order of senses—touching-touched—and things that happen on the level of bodies. Whereas when there is language, there is an account of experience because there is activity, with a reflectability that supposes a way of situating oneself in the world. Then you could understand the reaction of the man who was followed when he says: "You are going to record what I am doing." You are immediately put in the position of the interlocutor of intersubjectivity, as you said the other day.

**Jean Baudrillard:** That is correct. Do contradictions, paradoxes, or secrets require that there be no trace? At first, I would agree. I would say that a pact was broken, another reason for revenge.

Is writing a total betrayal of secrets or is it possible to slip a little bit of it into a nonaesthetic form? For me, it is not an aesthetic book but a book that remains secret, which keeps a trace of secrets.

I think you are basically correct but should we renounce the possibility of projecting an image of it, of being able to say it? There is certainly a way of saying it, a totally stupid and sacrilegious way to account for it. And there are probably various ways of keeping the secret. In the first things she did, there was a way of circling around the secret without divulging, decoding, or betraying it.

There may be no perfection in this case but the best she has done is nonetheless very close to the secret. The journal she kept during the operation was part of the following; publishing it is obviously something different.

The question raised is where the possibility of speaking about it stops. There must be a possibility of putting fate or alterity in this sense into action or in play, as long as their rules are followed. I think it is possible because otherwise she would never have staged it and would never have followed anyone. If she had not followed him, he would not have had a secret. She positions herself as the other's fate and she creates pure alterity; she had to do it. In order for someone to be another's fate, there must be a process of seduction with both total discretion and violence. Violence cannot be taken out; it has to be in play. The rules remain secret. You cannot say what the rule of this game is. She did not say it; she did not know it because she is extremely naïve, she did not look for it. I personally looked for it later but it didn't add anything. She has great naïveté but is capable of extraordinary artifice.

# SECRET ALTERITY

# 1

# Because Illusion and Reality

# are not Opposed

Photography is our exorcism. Primitive society had masks. Bourgeois society had mirrors. We have images.

We think that we control the world with technology. But with technology, the world controls us. It is a very surprising reversal.

You think that you take a picture of something because you like it—in fact, the scene wants its picture taken. You are only a part of its play. The subject is only the agent of the ironic appearance of things. The image is the ideal medium for the vast self-advertising of things and the world. It forces our imagination to withdraw, our passions to come out, breaking the mirror that we hold up, hypocritically, to capture them.

The miracle today is that appearances, which had long been willing servants, have turned on us, turned against us sovereignly through the very technology that we use to push them out. They now come from somewhere else, from their own place, from the heart of their banality. They irrupt from everywhere, joyfully multiplying themselves.

The pleasure of photography is objective excitement. Someone who has not experienced the objective elation of the image, at dawn, in a city, in a desert, will never understand the pataphysical delicacy of the world.

A thing wants to be photographed because it does not want to reveal its meaning or reflect itself. It wants to be captured directly, violated in place, illuminated in all its detail. It does not want to become an image so it can last but so it can disappear. And the subject is only a good medium if he or she enters into this game, if he or she exorcises his or her own glance and judgment, if he or she takes pleasure in his or her own absence.

The fabric of the object's details, its light and lines indicate this interruption of the subject, this intrusion of the world; it makes the suspense of photography. Through the image, the world imposes its discontinuity, its parceling, its artificial instantaneity. The photographic image is the purest image because it does not simulate time or movement and abides but the most rigorous irrealism. All of the other forms of the image (cinema, video, computer-generated, etc.) are only diluted forms of the pure image and its break with reality.

The intensity of the image corresponds to the extent of its denial of reality, to its invention of another stage. Making an object into an image means removing dimensions, one by one: weight, relief, odor, depth, time, continuity and, of course, meaning. The image receives its power to fascinate at the expense of this disembodiment. It becomes the medium of pure objectality, and it becomes transparent to a more subtle form of seduction.

Adding these dimensions back—relief, movement, emotion, idea, meaning and desire—to make it better or more real, or better simulated, is a complete misunderstanding of the image. And technology is caught in its own trap.

The desire to photograph may come from this realization: seen as a whole, in terms of meaning, the world is disappointing. Seen in detail and by surprise, it is always perfectly obvious.

Vertigo of the object's perpetual detail. Magical eccentricity of the detail. In photography, things connect by means of a technical operation that corresponds to the connections of their banality. One is an image for another image, a photo for another photo: contiguous fragments. No "world view," no glance: the refraction of the world, in its detail, on equal terms.

The absence of the world in each detail, like the absence of the subject sketched in each feature of a face. We can also reach this illumination of detail through a mental gymnastic or the subtleness of meaning. But technology does it effortlessly. It may be a trap.

Objects are such that their disappearance changes them into themselves. It is how they mislead us and make their illusion. But it is also how they remain faithful to themselves and how we should be faithful to them: in their minute details, in their precise figuration, in the sensuous illusion of their appearance and connection. Illusion is not opposed to reality, it is another, more subtle reality that envelops the first with the sign of its disappearance.

Each photographed object is only the trace left by the disappearance of the rest. It is an almost perfect crime, an almost complete resolution of the world that only allows the illusion of an object to shine, an object whose image then becomes an unsolvable puzzle. From this radical exception, you have an unparalleled view of the world.

Production is not the question. It is all in the art of disappearing. Only that which arrives in the mode of disappearance is truly other. But this disappearance must leave a trace, even the place where the Other, the world or the object appeared. It is in fact the only way for the Other to exist: through your disappearance.

"We shall be your favorite disappearing act!"

The only deep desire is the object desire (including the sexual object). Not the desire of what I miss or even of what (or who) misses me—which is more subtle—but the desire of what or who does not miss me, of what can exist very well without me. That which does not miss me is the Other, radical alterity.

The desire is always desire of this foreign perfection as well as the desire to shatter or undo it. We only have passion for what we want to share and destroy in its perfection and impunity.

Taking a photograph does not mean taking the world as an object but to make it become an object, uncovering the alterity buried beneath its so-called reality, making it emerge like a strange attractor and setting this strange attraction in an image.

Becoming once again a "thing among things," all foreign to each other yet complicit, opaque yet familiar—more than a universe of opposing, transparent subjects.

Photography brings us closest to a world without images or pure appearance.

The photographic image is dramatized in the struggle between the subject's will to impose an order, a vision, and the object's will to impose its discontinuity and immediateness. In the best case, the object wins and the photo-image is the image of a fractal world, with no equation or summons. It is therefore different from art and cinema, which in idea, vision and movement, always try to represent a totality.

Against the philosophy of the subject, of the look, of distance from the world to capture it better, the antiphilosophy of the object, of disconnection between objects, of the random succession of partial objects and details. Like a musical syncopation or the movement of particles.

Photography brings us closest to the fly with its faceted eye and broken line of flight.

For the object to be captured, the subject must divest itself of itself. But this is its final adventure, its last chance, the dispossession of the self in the reverberations of a world where it only occupies the blind spot of representation. The object has a much greater power to employ since it has not gone through the mirror stage and does not have to deal with its image, its identity, or its resemblance. Without desire and with nothing to say, it escapes commentary and interpretation.

If we can capture something of this dissemblance and singularity, something in the "real" world and in the very principle of reality changes.

The goal is to make the object the place of the subject's absence and disappearance instead of imposing the presence and representation of the subject on it. The object can be a situation, a light, a living creature. The main thing is for the overly well-wrought machinery of representation to break (along with the moral and philosophical dialectics attached to it) and to have the world emerge as an indissoluble certainty through a pure event of the image.

It is a reversal of the mirror. Until now, the subject was the mirror of representation. The object was its content. Now the object says: "I shall be your mirror!"

Photography has an obsessive, temperamental, ecstatic and narcissistic aspect. It is a solitary activity. The photographic image is discontinuous, punctual, unpredictable and irreparable like the state of things at a given moment. Every retouch, every regret, every staging takes on an abominably aesthetic quality. The solitude of the photographic subject, in space and time, is correlative to the solitude of the object and its temperamental silence.

The object must be set, watched intensely and immobilized by the look. The object does not pose; the operator must hold his or her breath to empty time and body. But also mentally keep his or herself from breathing and think of nothing so that the mental surface is as pure as the film. Not taking him or herself as a representative being but as an object that works in its own cycle without concern for the staging, in a kind of delirious circumspection of self and object. This enchantment can also be found in games—the excitement of going beyond one's own image into kind of a happy fate. You play and you do not play at the same time. Emptiness in the self and around the self occurs the same way, through a kind of initiatory enfolding. You do no longer project yourself in an image—you produce the world as a singular event, without commentary.

Photography is not a real-time image. It keeps the moment of the negative, the suspense of the negative. This slight discrepancy allows the image to exist as such, as an illusion that is different from the real world. This slight discrepancy gives it the discreet charm of a previous life unfolding in real time, something digital images and video lack. In computer-generated images, reality is already gone. For that reason, there are truly images.

There is a form of astonishment in photography, of suspense, of phenomenal immobility that interrupts the rush of events. The freeze frame freezes the world. The suspension is never definitive, however, because photos refer to each other and the only end of the image is in images. Yet each image is distinct from the others.

Through this distinction and secret complicity, photography regains the aura that it lost with cinema. But cinema can also rediscover this quality of the image—complicit in and yet foreign to narration—since it has its own stasis animated by all the energy of movement—crystallizing an entire unfolding in a fixed image according to a principle of condensation that counters the principle of high dilution and dispersion of all of our current images. In Godard's films for example.

It is rare for a text to show off the same obviousness, the same instantaneity, the same magic as a shadow, a light, a material. However, in Nabokov and Gombrowicz, for example, writing sometimes finds something of the material, objectal autonomy of things without quality, the erotic power and supernatural disorder of a null world.

True immobility is not an inert body but the stillness of a weight on the end of a pendulum whose oscillations have just stopped and which still vibrates imperceptibly. It is the immobility of time in the instant, of photographic "instantaneity" behind which lies the idea of movement, but only the idea. The image is there to make one respect movement without ever showing it, which would dispel its illusion. Things dream of this immobility and so do we. Cinema is now concentrating on it more and more, with its nostalgia of slow motion and freeze frames as the highest moments of drama.

The same is true of silence. The paradox of television may be that it renewed the charm of the image's silence.

The silence of photography. One of its most precious qualities in contrast with television and cinema, which always have to be silenced, though without success. The silence of the image that needs no (or should not need any) commentary. But there is also the silence of the object that is ripped from the cumbersome and deafening context of the real world. Whatever the noise and violence that surround it, a photo gives the object back its immobility and quiet. It creates the equivalent of the desert, phenomenal isolation, in the midst of urban confusion. It is the only way to travel through cities silently, to move through the world in silence.

Photography accounts for the state of the world in our absence. The lens explores this absence. It explores this absence even in faces or bodies filled with emotion. Our best photographs are of those for whom the other does not exist or no longer exists—primitive people, miserable people, objects. Only the inhuman is photogenic. This is the price of a reciprocal astonishment and thus a complicity between us and the world, and between the world and us.

Human beings are too sentimental. Even animals and plants are too sentimental. Only objects have no sexual or sentimental aura.

There is therefore no need to violate them in cold blood to photograph them. Because they have no problems with resemblance, they are remarkably identical to themselves. Through technology, you can only add to the magical certainty of their indifference, to the innocence of their staging and put what they incarnate into relief: the objective illusion and subjective disillusion of the world.

It is very difficult to photograph individuals or faces. Photographic precision is impossible for someone whose psychological precision leaves so much to desire. Every human being is the locus of such a staging, the place of such a complex (de)construction that the lens removes its character in spite of his or herself. Its meaning has changed so much that it is almost impossible to separate it to find the secret form of its absence.

They say that there is always a moment to catch when the most banal or mysterious creature reveals its secret identity. But its secret alterity is more interesting. Instead of looking for the identity behind the mask, we should look for the mask behind the identity—the figure that haunts us and makes us turn away from our identity—the hidden divinity that haunts each and every one of us for a moment, at some point in time.

For objects, savages, animals, and primitive peoples, alterity and singularity are certain. An animal has no identity and yet is not alienated. It is a stranger to itself and its own ends. They have the charm of creatures who do not know their own image but who therefore enjoy an organic familiarity with their own body and all others. If we can rediscover this connivance and strangeness, then we are closer to the poetic quality of alterity: the quality of dreams and active (REM) sleep, with identity equated to deep sleep.

Objects and primitive peoples are ahead of us in photogenic terms. Free of psychology and introspection, they are able to keep their seduction in front of the lens. Free of representation, they are able to keep their presence whole. This is much less sure for the subject. The subject—is it the price of intelligence or a sign of stupidity?—most often succeeds in denying his or her alterity and exists within the limits of his or her identity. What subjects need to do is to make themselves more mysterious to themselves, and make human beings in general more strange (or foreign) to each other. This does not mean taking them as subjects but making them objects, making them other. In other words, it means taking them for what they are.

"You must capture people in their relationship to themselves, in their silence." (H. Cartier-Bresson)

We live for a large part in an arrangement of will and representation, but the crux of the story lies elsewhere. Everyone is certainly there with his or her desire and will but, secretly, decisions and thoughts come from somewhere else; originality lies in this bizarre interface. Originality is not in recognition in the mirror or in the lens that wants to recognize him or her. Resemblance is always the trap. The greatness of the image lies in defying resemblance, in seeking elsewhere the things that come from elsewhere.

There was a time when the confrontation with the lens was dramatic, when images were at stake, when they were a magical, dangerous reality. There was no complacency with images—fear, defiance, pride—which gave every turn-of-the-century farmer or bourgeois surrounded by his family the same deadly or fierce seriousness of a primitive. Their being freezes, their eyes dilate in front of the image, they spontaneously act dead. And the lens becomes wild as well. All of the promiscuity of the photographer and his or her object is excluded (as opposed to contemporary practices). The distance is insurmountable, and photography is the technical equivalent of Segalen's radical exoticism. There is a veritable nobility in the photographic event, like a distant echo of the primitive shock of cultures.

In the heroic period, the photographic relationship is a duel and death is possible. The cadaverous stillness of the object, his or her absence of expression (but not of character) is just as powerful as mobility of the lens, which it holds in the balance. The destiny he or she has in mind, his or her mental universe directly imprints the film—an effect that is just as strong today as it was a century ago when the photo was taken. We capture the wild or the primitive in our lens, but they imagine us.

This death, this virtual disappearance of the object in the heroic period is still present in the anthropological heart of the image, according to Barthes. The "punctum" is the figure of the void, of absence opposed to the "studium," which is the context of meaning and reference. The void at the heart of the image gives it the magic and power that are usually pushed out by significations.

In festivals, galleries, museums and exhibits, images overflow with messages, testimonies, aesthetic sentimentality, and stereotypes of recognition. They prostitute the image to its meaning, to what it wants to communicate; the image is taken hostage by the one who took it or by current media events. In the current proliferation of images, death and violence are everywhere; but they are pathetic, ideological, spectacular. They are nothing like the "punctum" with its fatal arrangement internal to the image that has been pushed out.

Instead of the image symbolically containing death, death closes on the image (in the external form of an exhibit, museum, or the cultural necropolises that exalt photograph.).

The image is off-camera, out of the frame. Photographic direction, either inside the image or the institution, is meaningless. Buried under commentary, walled in by aesthetic praise, condemned to the plastic surgery of the museum, the internal hallucination of the image is moribund. There is not even a "stadium" opposed to a "punctum"; there is only a circulating medium. And the fundamentally dangerous form of the image is resolved in the cultural circulation of masterpieces.

I regret the aestheticization of photography. I regret that it became one of the Fine Arts and has entered the realm of culture. The photographic image, with its technological essence, came below and beyond aesthetics and was thus a substantial revolution in our mode of representation. Its emergence called into question art's aesthetic monopoly on the image. Today, the opposite is occurring: art is devouring photography.

Photography is deeply inscribed in another dimension. Not an aesthetic dimension but something like *trompe-l'œil*, which has been present throughout the history of art while remaining indifferent to art's upheavals. *Trompe-l'œil* is only apparently realist; in fact, it is tied to the obviousness of the world and to such a minute resemblance that it becomes magical. *Trompe-l'œil*, like photography, retains something of the magic of the image, of the world's radical illusion. A wild, irreducible form closer to the origins and tribulations of representation—connected to the appearance and obviousness of the world, albeit a misleading obviousness—which is therefore opposed to any realist vision and still today less viable in terms of judgment and taste than in terms of pure fascination.

Through its irrealist play with technology, through its cutting out, its stillness, its silence, its phenomenological reduction of movement and sometimes color, through these aspects, photography imposes itself as the purest and most artificial image. It is not beautiful, it is worse and thereby takes on the force of an object in a world from which the aesthetic principle is fading.

Technology gives photography its unique character. Through technicality, our world reveals itself to be radically nonobjective. The photographic lens [*objectif*] paradoxically reveals the inobjectivity of the world—that something that will not be solved by analysis or resemblance.

Technology takes us beyond resemblance. It takes us to the heart of the *trompe-l'œil* of reality. Our view of technology is transformed at the same time. It becomes the site of a double game like an enlarging mirror of illusion and forms. The world and technological devices are complicit; objective technology and the power of the object converge. Photography is the art of slipping into this complicity. Not to control the process but to play with it, to make evident that the game is not over.

The world in itself does not resemble anything. As a concept and a discourse, it relates to many other things; as a pure object, it cannot be identified.

The photographic operation is a type of reflex or automatic writing of the obviousness of the world, which is not one.

In the generic illusion of the image, there is no problem of reality. It disappears in its movement, going immediately and spontaneously beyond true and false, beyond reality and illusion, beyond good and evil.

The image is not a medium that we must learn to use correctly. It is what it is; it is beyond all of our moral calculations. It is immoral in its essence; the becoming-image of the world is a becoming-immoral. It is up to us to escape our representation and become the immoral vector of the image. It is up to us to become objects again, to become others again in a seductive relationship with the world.

Let the silent complicity between object and lens, between appearances and technology, between the physical quality of light and the metaphysical complexity of the technological devices unfold without bringing in vision or meaning.

Because the object sees us. The object dreams us. The world reflects us, the world thinks us. This is the fundamental rule.

Having the object do all of the work is the magic of photography. Photographers would never admit it and contend that all originality comes in their own inspiration, their own photographic interpretation of the world. By confusing their subjective vision with the reflex miracle of the photographic act, they can only make photos that are bad, or too good.

# 2

# What They Looked
# Like Photographed

If you are someone who thinks that photography must free itself from any obligation of meaning, from any imposed signification, then the in-significant naturally becomes its object. More precisely, in a world overflowing with all possible meanings, photography must bring out the insignificance that lies at the center of the object—it must find the void at the heart of the image, as Warhol said. The different uses of photography call metaphysics into question and reject the metaphysics of the image.

Our superstitious view of reality leads us to believe that the world presents itself to us under the (specious, superficial) guise of appearance and that truth, the deep meaning of things, waits behind the mask or veil of appearances. The opposite is true. Meaning imposes itself on us first; the empire of meaning is our true morality. The obviousness of meaning masks the obviousness of the senses.

In fact, appearances are nothing less than evident. We should instead say that they "fall under meaning," in the sense that they succumb to it.

That is why I see photography and the radical, radically "insignificant" use of the image as a true public service. It relieves us of excess meaning and, against our obsessive tendency to interpret everything, to give everything meaning, gives us the opposite tendency to resist the excess production of meaning through images (let alone thought). Photography lets us enter a constellation of secrets, emptiness, and silence that foil any attempts at interpretation and act through manifestation, indecision and surprise.

As a result, to the extent that we are (still) in it, the world is never as it is. The world is only objectively real when there is no one there to see it. Our affectation to provide a mirror image of the world or to express reality faithfully is an illusion.

From the start, photography has contributed to reinforcing or grounding this superstition of the world as it is because of the realistic precision of photos. Finally, a "real" picture of the world. (At the very same moment, in the 19th century, emerging technology began to dissolve this reality into increasing abstraction, leading today to the virtual reality from which reality has disappeared).

At best, the photographic image is a trace, perhaps a nostalgic trace, of something disappearing. The vast profusion of images today plays a decisive role in this disappearance of reality. The violence of the image, the violence done to reality by images occurs when images are reduced to nothing more than the shadow of reality. This violence is correlative to the violence done to images by meaning, by media staging and by all of the determinations we impose on them. It is particularly true when photography is reduced to being nothing more than the technological medium for an undiscoverable reality.

We are wrong about photography if we consider it to be art in the conventional sense or a kind of recording device. On the contrary, it requires a magical rethinking of the image and an initiatory approach.

This position does not take reality for granted. It approaches reality as it emerges, still ambivalent, "poorly lateralized," before it has the time to signify. It separates photography from all of the commanding interventions, documentaries, ideologies, moralities and aesthetics that represent the violence done to images and the world as it is (or appears to be) in the name of a world that should be.

Of course, these considerations are themselves an attempt to interpret, to give meaning and they therefore contradict what they say. Commenting on images that want no commentary is perfectly useless. The same contradiction is found in representing something that does not want to be represented. And it is all the more paradoxical because it is a "fuzzy tendency," a "vague trend" without any exact reference or specific objective that nonetheless aims to distance itself from the conventional use of images.

There is, however, a kind of philosophy behind this "trend." Behind the "vague" there is the sense of the impossibility of precisely representing reality, the impossibility of accounting for its fluidity, ephemerality, and imprecision. There is a sense of being and bearing witness to this impossibility and action taken to capture its movement and mode of appearance through anamorphosis and improvisation. All images are different, and freely so, but they secretly converge at a level other than the level of witnessing or stories. In any case, there could only be "objective reality" in a world from which we are absent, a world of pure objects from which we have disappeared. Appearances would be gone with us, for who needs appearances in a world without gazes?

Photography is meaningless if it only reflects the subject's photographic desire and not the world's desire to be photographed and seen but equally to see and impose itself on the gaze. This reciprocity in inscribed in the medium, in the camera itself. It is never just a technological agent but an invitation to the world to produce itself as an image. If we do not feel that reciprocity, then photography is just an empty, unilateral technique.

It is a delicate operation with a subtle play between subject, object and medium. Who will come out on top? There is the chance that the object will win in the form of objective realism (documentary, reportage) and the contrary chance that the subject will impose his or her style and point of view (the photographer's "style," "universe," or even "work") But there is a third risk: the risk that the medium itself, the machine, imposes its law (or its desire, if we can say machines have desires). We have known since William Flusser that a camera, a photographic machine left to its own devices and internal logic only tends towards one thing: exhausting all of its possibilities. In other words, functioning non-stop no matter what the occasion, scenario or actors. Completing its program without hesitation—at the expense of subject and object, who become mere technical agents of the camera's "will."

This explains the automatic proliferation of satellite images where the photos (but are they still photos?) are just scans of the world's banality adjusted by remote control.

Digital images best portray the risk of endless images lacking the reciprocity of the world's view of us and our view of the world. In this sense, digital images are one extreme of the photographic medium but also its liquidation. These countless images are not made to be seen but to pass by the world without seeing it. If photography, as some have said, is a powerful aphrodisiac, then its digital use is just an extended form of pornography. Maybe the camera is also an instrument of perversion: allowing those exiled from their own existence to collect details about their life so that nothing that happened is lost. Or it could be a desperate form of witnessing.

The most exciting aspect of photography, however, is the way objects appear. In the desert, in a city or on a trip, the way objects appear, the phenomenal obviousness of the world is a source of absolute pleasure (whereas analysis and writing are a source of anxiety). Photographic desire comes from this, aiming beyond reality for objects in their poetic instantaneity. It is more like a kind of phenomenology.

The desire to photograph is the opposite of the desire to signify at all costs, to bear witness, or to inform. It is closer to astonishment and illusion. Closer to disappearance as well, since something does not want to become an image in order to endure but to disappear. The photographic gaze, or the gaze of light, sits literally on the surface of things and illustrates their fragmentary appearance for a very brief moment of time. Taking a photograph does not mean accounting for the objective world, it means making it into an object, letting it impose its immediacy and discontinuity, its temporary, unpredictable, and irreparable nature through the happy fate of appearances.

Capturing things in their pure obviousness is a dream. The subject is the main obstacle, with his or her desire to represent, to signify at all costs. A pervasive information and communication morality rules the production and profusion of images today (on television and in the media, for example). But it is not "visual," as Serge Daney would say. Photography is something different. Detachment and a certain objective casualness are necessary to bring out the way things appear without forcing them. Only when we give images back their singularity can reality recover its true image. Through images, we must tear reality away from the principle of reality.

Simply put, photography gives phenomena their importance while calling our presence into question. We could even say that photography records the world in our absence. Through images, things, while giving us a sign, tell us that they do not need us to exist totally in their form, light, and metamorphosis. Images are the trace of a philosophical experience: the experience of the radical indifference of the world. Thus its affinity with stillness, deserts, and silence. Photography is always desert-like, deserted by meaning. Deserts are meaningless too; they are another stage: networks of light and fossils of inhuman intelligence. Thus photography has always been associated, from its origins, with traveling shots in space, in the desert of the cities, and in the space-time of travel.

A true photo is never far from the void—it empties the space around it and freezes the world in a frame. It has to be exceptional; it must be used with care. Unfortunately, in our constant flux, the worst thing for us today is the impossibility of a world without images, a world that is not constantly caught up in image-feedback, captured, filmed, and photographed before being seen. At the heart of this whirlwind lies the disappearance of the image, of the image as illusion, as an exception, as a primitive scene.

More and more images represent ad nauseam the same events; they overlap, form series, and negate each other. In this visual flux, they do not even have time to become images. They lose their freedom most of all. In the promiscuity of the visual flux, each one takes space from the others. But images must be free and sovereign; each one's aura should eclipse many others—since images are engaged in a constant duel. If they are alive, then they must follow the laws of living creatures: selection and elimination. We are headed in the opposite direction today, especially with digital images where the parade of images resembles gene sequencing.

In the reign of photographic expressionism, the world can only wait to be witness to a subject's existence and a subject's gaze. Maintaining this position is an utter mistake; even "exposure" is not essential to photographic vision. Each second, there are multiple scenes, lights and events that we photograph *mentally*—without counting the ones we would dream of photographing (we even dream of photographing our dreams). If the camera is a technological extension of the eye, the photographic image is an extension of the gaze: not only an objective perception, but a vision. Sometimes, but only sometimes, there is a picture that materializes this vision of things—not things as they are in themselves, but such as photography changes them into themselves: what they look like *photographed.*

# ALSO FROM SEMIOTEXT(E)

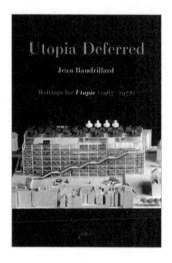

## UTOPIA DEFERRED
### Writings from Utopie (1967–1978)
Jean Baudrillard, Translated by Stuart Kendall

The Utopie group was born in 1966 at Henri Lefebvre's house in the Pyrenees. The eponymous journal edited by Hubert Tonka brought together sociologists Jean Baudrillard, René Lourau, and Catherine Cot, architects Jean Aubert, Jean-Paul Jungmann, Antoine Stinco, and landscape architect Isabelle Auricoste. Over the next decade, both in theory and in practice, the group articulated a radical ultra-leftist critique of architecture, urbanism, and everyday life. *Utopia Deferred* collects all of the essays Jean Baudrillard published in Utopie as well as recent interview with the author.

6 x 9 • 328 pages • ISBN-13: 978-1-58435-033-0 • $17.95

## THE CONSPIRACY OF ART
### Manifestos, Texts, Interviews
Jean Baudrillard, Introduction by Sylvère Lotringer

In *The Conspiracy of Art*, Baudrillard questions the privilege attached to art by its practitioners. Art has lost all desire for illusion: feeding back endlessly into itself, it has turned its own vanishment into an art unto itself. Far from lamenting the "end of art," Baudrillard celebrates art's new function within the process of insider-trading. Spiraling from aesthetic nullity to commercial frenzy, art has become transaesthetic, like society as a whole.

Conceived and edited by life-long Baudrillard collaborator Sylvère Lotringer, *The Conspiracy of Art* presents Baudrillard's writings on art in a complicitous dance with politics, economics, and media.

6 x 9 • 232 pages • ISBN-13: 978-1-58435-028-6 • $14.95

## FORGET FOUCAULT
Jean Baudrillard, Introduction by Sylvère Lotringer

In 1976, Jean Baudrillard sent this essay to the French magazine *Critique*, of which Michel Foucault was an editor. Foucault was asked to reply, but remained silent. *Oublier Foucault* (1977) made Baudrillard instantly infamous in France. It was a devastating revisitation of Foucault's recent *History of Sexuality* and of his entire œuvre. Also an attack on those philosophers, like Gilles Deleuze and Félix Guattari, who believed that 'desire' could be revolutionary. In Baudrillard's eyes, desire and power were exchangeable, so desire had no place in Foucault. There is no better introduction to Baudrillard's polemical approach to culture than these pages where he dares Foucault to meet the challenge of his own thought. First published in 1987 in America with a dialogue with Sylvère Lotringer : *Forget Baudrillard*, this new edition contains a new introduction by Lotringer revisiting the ideas and impact of this singular book.

6 x 9 • 144 pages • ISBN-13: 978-1-58435-041-5 • $14.95

## FATAL STRATEGIES
Jean Baudrillard, Introduction by Dominic Pettman

In this shimmering manifesto against dialectics, Jean Baudrillard constructs a condemnatory ethics of the "false problem." One foot in social science, the other in speculation about the history of ideas, this text epitomizes the assault that Baudrillard has made on the history of Western philosophy. Posing such anti-questions as "Must we put information on a diet?" Baudrillard cuts across historical and contemporary space with profound observations on American corporations, arms build-up, hostage-taking, transgression, truth, and the fate of theory itself. Not only an important map of Baudrillard's continuing examination of evil, this essay is also a profound critique of 1980s American politics at the time when the author was beginning to have his incalculable effect on a generation of this country's artists and theorists.

6 x 9 • 232 pages • ISBN-13: 978-1-58435-061-3 • $14.95